Ralph
NADER

Ralph NADER
MAN WITH A MISSION

NANCY BOWEN

Twenty-First Century Books
Brookfield, Connecticut

For Bob: my love, my friend,
and my personal copy editor

Cover photograph courtesy of © Reuters NewMedia Inc./Corbis

Photographs courtesy of AP/Wide World Photos: pp. 12, 71, 88,
92, 106; The Hartford Courant: p. 15 (file photo/Jack Bourque);
© Claire Nader: pp. 17, 20; © Sonja Zinke: pp. 19, 23, 87; Princeton
University Library: p. 26 (University Archives, Department of Rare
Books and Special Collections); Harvard Law School: p. 33
(Art & Visual Materials, Special Collections Department);
© Bettmann/Corbis: pp. 46, 74; TimePix: p. 54 (© John Zimmerman);
Corbis/Sygma: p. 91 (© Ira Wyman); © Lawrence Hannafin: p. 121;
The Junior Statesmen Foundation: p. 124

Library of Congress Cataloging-in-Publication Data
Bowen, Nancy.
Ralph Nader : man with a mission / Nancy Bowen.
p. cm.
Includes bibliographical references and index.
Summary: A biography of the consumer advocate who has devoted
his life to crusading for citizens' rights, and who ran as the Green
Party's presidential candidate in 2000.
ISBN 0-7613-2365-1 (lib. bdg.)
1. Nader, Ralph—Juvenile literature. 2. Consumer affairs directors—
United States—Biography—Juvenile literature. 3. Lobbyists—United
States—Juvenile literature. 4. Consumer protection—United States—
Juvenile literature. 5. Political campaigns—United States—Juvenile
literature. 6. Traffic safety—United States—Juvenile literature.
[1. Nader, Ralph. 2. Presidential candidates. 3. Consumer affairs
directors. 4. Lobbyists. 5. Consumer protection.] I. Title.
HC110.C63 N322 2001
343.7307'1'092—dc21
[B] 2001041464

Published by Twenty-First Century Books
A Division of The Millbrook Press, Inc.
2 Old New Milford Road
Brookfield, Connecticut 06804

I thank Sally and Larry Hannafin and Claire Nader for sharing their knowledge and reflections about Ralph Nader. And I am especially grateful to Ralph Nader for the time he spent answering my questions about his life, his work, and the challenges of the United States in the twenty-first century.

Contents

Ralph
NADER

With over 100 pages of new material

Unsafe at Any Speed

The designed-in dangers of the American automobile

Ralph Nader

An edition of Unsafe at Any Speed

Introduction

◈◈◈Buried on page 68 of the November 30, 1965, edition of *The New York Times* was a one-column article headlined: "Lawyer Charges Auto Safety Lag—In Book, He Blames Traffic Safety Establishment." The article marked the publication of *Unsafe at Any Speed*, the little book that would launch a revolution known as consumer activism in the United States. Its author was an unknown thirty-one-year-old Washington lawyer and freelance writer named Ralph Nader, who had testified before a Senate subcommittee looking into automobile safety.

Although the book received favorable reviews in the national press, the "traffic safety establishment" that Nader so sharply criticized—Detroit automakers, Akron tire manufacturers, the National Safety Council, and the American Automobile Association—took no official notice of the new book. Unofficially, however, the folks at General Motors were very interested in the young lawyer. Within four months of the book's publication, the curiosity of General Motors' legal staff had made Nader front-page news all across the country, and *Unsafe at Any Speed* was on the bestseller lists.

Nader testifies on March 22, 1966, before the Senate Government Operations Subcommittee, which was looking into automobile safety.

"GM Acknowledges Investigating Critic" said the page one headline in *The New York Times* on March 9, 1966. The giant automaker had hired private investigators to spy on Nader, the man whose book had alerted the nation to the dangers of the GM sports car called the Corvair. The investigators were looking for something shocking in his personal life, something they could use to discredit him. They questioned his friends and associates, including elementary-school classmates and the high-school principal from his hometown in Connecticut. They followed Nader so closely and so frequently that he knew he was being watched. At the U. S. Capitol, Senate security guards spotted the investigators following Nader and stopped them from entering the building. But the investigation found nothing that would damage him; GM operatives were unhappy with findings that indicated he was "a charming intellectual . . . an Eagle Scout type. . . ."[1]

Nader publicly accused GM of spying, harassment, and intimidation. At first, the automaker denied the charges, but within days, company chairman James Roche issued a statement apologizing to Nader, but claiming that the company was only carrying out a "routine investigation." Two weeks later, Roche testified before a Senate subcommittee and admitted that the investigation was much more extensive than he had originally stated. Once again he apologized to Nader.[2]

The book, the GM investigation, and the Senate hearings on auto safety combined to make Ralph Nader a household name and a folk hero. He was truly an American David taking on the Goliath of American industry—General Motors and the automobile manufacturers.

∾∾∾

To most observers, his rise to fame was sudden and spectacular, but in fact Ralph Nader had been preparing for this role for most of his young life.

Chapter One "Did you believe what you were told or did you question?"

～～～To begin to know Ralph Nader, it is important to understand the culture into which he was born and the values of the parents who raised him. The Naders were *not* a typical American family.

Nader's father, Nathra, left his native Lebanon when he was nineteen years old and set sail for America. Lebanon was then part of the Ottoman Empire, and Nathra felt that he had no freedom under Turkish rule. Later, he often told his children that when he sailed past the Statue of Liberty—America's symbol of freedom—he took it very seriously.

Nathra worked in the United States for several years, saved his money, and returned to Lebanon in 1925. There he met and married Rose Bouziane, a school-teacher. One of the treaties that had officially ended World War I (1914–1918), the Treaty of Sèvres, had taken Lebanon away from the Ottoman Empire and placed it under French rule. So once again Nathra felt that he

Protesting congressional pay raises, octogenarian Nathra Nader (center) leads a march through downtown Winsted, Connecticut, in 1977.

had to flee Lebanon in order to find freedom. He took his bride to America. They eventually settled in the small town of Winsted in northwestern Connecticut.

There, Rose and Nathra would establish a restaurant and raise their four children: son, Shafeek, two daughters, Claire and Laura, and Ralph, the youngest, born on February 27, 1934. Claire Nader recalls that their family was different from those of her playmates and neighbors. "We were bicultural and bilingual, frequently speaking Arabic at home. My parents valued their Lebanese heritage, and they taught us to respect that culture as well as the best in the American culture into which we were born."[1]

Nathra Nader had left his homeland in protest over government domination. So, for him and his family, freedom and democracy were more than abstract ideas. He and his wife fervently believed that democracy was a great responsibility. And one of those responsibilities was to speak out *against* injustices of any kind and *for* the rights of individuals. Nathra believed that freedom of speech must be practiced if it is to be of value.

In addition to the Naders' respect for freedom, they had a strong sense of responsibility toward others. "We were raised to make things better," Claire says. "If we saw something that wasn't right or fair, we had to do something about it. If a neighbor needed help, we helped. If something in the town needed fixing, we tried to fix it. We were all very tuned-in to this; we just learned it through osmosis—from experiencing our parents living in this way. Our parents expected us to do the right thing, to listen, and to learn from the example they set."[2]

Nathra Nader was a concerned citizen. He was concerned about his family, his community, his adopted country, and international politics. Early on, he and Rose instilled this interest into the children through nightly dinner-table discussions. He posed hypothetical "What if . . . ?" questions to the children to stimulate their thinking on every conceivable subject. Nathra was

Young Ralph with his mother, Rose, outside their home in Winsted, Connecticut.

an avid reader and a man of strong opinions. He challenged his children to follow his lead. "They conversed with us about whatever was on their minds," Claire recalls. "This is the highest compliment a parent can pay. It didn't matter what age we were, we were old enough to know that we were having a discussion with our parents. It was what we said that counted, not what age we were. These conversations were very stimulating for us as children—more stimulating than going to school."[3]

Nathra prodded the children at the dinner-table discussions and taught them to question and debate every issue. He wanted to know what they thought, but they had to stand their ground. "Even the youngest had to defend his position," Claire says. "We were not allowed to run under fire."[4]

According to Nader biographer Robert Buckhorn, those childhood dinner-table discussions left a lasting mark on Ralph Nader. "He is intense when he pleads a cause or makes a point, but he remains quick to smile and possesses a low-keyed wit that keeps his usually serious subjects from becoming so depressing that they turn the audience off."[5]

Rose Nader remembers that her husband's favorite topics for discussion were political: colonialism, taxation, stifling of small business by big business, education for citizenship, and the basic needs of the community. Her concerns centered on food and health, contaminants in the environment, children's welfare, and nuclear war.

The Naders' desire to have their children think and question did not end at the family dinner table. Nathra would often greet a child returning from school with questions such as: "Well, what did you learn in school today? Did you just believe what you were told or did you *question?* Did you believe or did you *think?*"

∾∾∾

But Ralph Nader's childhood was not all intellectual discussion—his earliest childhood memories are of running in the woods, watching his father mow the lawn, and helping his mother in the kitchen. When he was older, he took long trips on his bicycle, hiked, and went sledding in the winter. He had a newspaper route, played basketball, sandlot baseball, and he became an avid New York Yankees fan.

Claire remembers that the four children loved to hike up the hill that rose behind their white, ten-room house to the 60-foot (18-meter)-high Soldiers Monument: "We'd take our lunch, and each one of us would sit under one of the four arches of the monument. We'd

Soldiers Monument in Winsted, Connecticut

Young Ralph with his older brother, Shafeek, around 1939

Ralph, about age ten, proudly displays produce from his World War II victory garden.

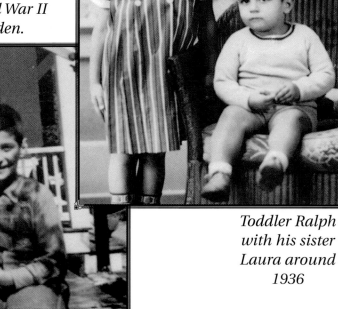

Toddler Ralph with his sister Laura around 1936

eat, and talk, and we became friends, not just siblings. Our pleasures were really quite simple, because our parents didn't believe in material things."[6]

Nor did Rose Nader believe in a lot of planned activities for children. She thought children should have rest and quiet time. Claire says that turned out to be a good thing because "in quiet time, you find out who you are."[7]

From the age of five, Ralph went with his father to the local courthouse to watch cases being tried. Nathra believed that lawyers could make a greater difference in the world than any other profession—an opinion that Ralph would later share. Ralph also went with his father and brother to local town meetings, which, in typical New England fashion, were often the scene of heated debates about local issues. Frequently, the most heated debater was Nathra Nader himself.

Ralph was an excellent student and an avid reader. His brother Shafeek—eight years his senior—prepared reading lists for him (Claire typed them up), and then discussed the books with Ralph after he had read them. With his interest in social issues ignited by the family dinner-table discussions, Ralph began reading books by early twentieth-century journalists and authors who used their writings to alert the nation to exploitation by big business. Called "muckrakers," they included Ida Tarbell, a journalist who investigated and wrote an exposé of the oil trust, *A History of the Standard Oil Company*, and Upton Sinclair, author of *The Jungle*, an exposé of Chicago's slaughterhouses.

When he was fourteen, Ralph came upon a pile of back issues of the *Congressional Record* stashed away in his school library. The *Congressional Record* is the official publication of the proceedings of the U.S. Congress, including transcripts of all discussions and debates. It is published every day that Congress is in session. Each issue contains many thousands of words, and the volumes are quite cumbersome. No one else in the school read them or wanted them, but Ralph lugged them home and announced to his mother that he intended to read every word of every issue. It was his first introduction to the workings of the Congress of the United States.

༄ ༄ ༄

Young Nader learned about issues such as social responsibility, good citizenship, and freedom of speech at the family dinners and through his reading. But he learned about people in the family-run restaurant, which Nathra had named Highland Arms because it was in the "high lands" of Connecticut and because he wanted his establishment to be the "arms" that reached out to the community, a place where both the body and the mind were nourished.

It was not a place to have a quiet meal. Nathra had opinions and he shared them with his customers. "You couldn't get out of the restaurant without talking to him," says Claire, "and the conversation was never just about the weather."[8] Townspeople said that at the Highland Arms you got a five-cent cup of coffee and a dollar's worth of conversation.

The family shared responsibility for running the restaurant, and Ralph often worked there. He especially liked working behind the counter or at the cash register where he could talk to the customers. Unlike his father who volunteered his opinions, Ralph asked many questions and listened carefully to the opinions and concerns of the patrons. And they did have concerns. During those years, Winsted was not an idyllic New

Main Street, Winsted, Connecticut

England town. It was a mill and factory town of about ten thousand people facing economic problems. The Great Depression had slowed the mills along the Mad River, and the number of factories had dropped by two-thirds since the beginning of the twentieth century. "Everyone who came to the restaurant was fed," recalls Claire, "those with money and those without. And during the Depression, there were many who were without."[9]

In addition to the factory workers, both employed and unemployed, who frequented the restaurant, there were salesmen passing through, and lawyers and their clients from the courthouse. Ralph listened to them all and absorbed what they had to say.

Ralph Nader passed his childhood and teen years in that stimulating, activist setting. Recently he recalled those years: "It was a very civically responsible upbringing. Basically, my parents said that the other side of freedom is civic responsibility. So we were always encouraged to participate and to try to improve our community and not be passive onlookers or bystanders. . . ."[10]

∾∾∾

Rose and Nathra Nader did their job well. The last thing their son Ralph would ever be is "a passive onlooker or bystander."

Chapter Two "... Vision coupled with enormous determination"

ᗑᗑᗑIn the autumn of 1951, Ralph Nader entered Princeton University in New Jersey. He chose Princeton because it had an excellent Oriental studies department, offered a Middle East studies program, and was home to the Woodrow Wilson School for Public and International Affairs. Clearly, his bicultural background and far-flung reading interests had set him on a course of study that was global in nature. Princeton offered him a scholarship, but his father refused, saying the money should go to a student whose parents couldn't afford the tuition. Nathra had saved for his children's education.

The variety of Nader's interests at Princeton reflected his background and offered a preview of things to come. He majored in Oriental studies and mastered the Chinese language. But he also mastered Russian and Spanish. In his junior year he received a scholarship to study agricultural problems in Europe. During one summer vacation he visited Native American reservations in New Mexico, Arizona, and California. He studied the poverty and living conditions

The blurb under Nader's Princeton yearbook photo relates that he was a member of the Prospect Club and his "activities included I.A.A. football, Whig-Clio, Pre-Law Society, and the Middle East Club." His senior thesis was titled "Some Problems in the Economic Development of Lebanon."

of Native Americans and was struck by the mental state of the people, many of whom felt hopeless and helpless in their struggles with the U.S. government.

Nader was considered by many of his classmates to be a "grind" at Princeton. Not only did he study hard and do well on his assigned courses, but he also audited extra classes just because he loved to learn. This did not endear him to his classmates, but, then again, he was not very happy with them, either. He thought that many of them were too content with the "Gentleman's C" grade average and too preoccupied with what clothes they wore, what cars they drove, and who their friends were. Some of his peers thought his reluctance to join in conversations about such interests meant that he was shy. He wasn't shy, he just didn't care to waste his time talking about matters that were of no importance to him. His friends knew that if he started talking about politics or social issues, he could go on endlessly.

Most of the young men on campus dressed the same way: tweed jackets, white shirts, khaki pants, and white buckskin shoes. This bothered Nader, who thought that this conformity showed a lack of individuality—just the opposite of the "think for yourself" way in which he was raised. One day, to protest the sheeplike dress code, Nader went to class in a bathrobe and slippers.[1]

In ten years, the 1960s would see the Ivy League look give way to tie-dyed shirts, torn jeans, long hair, sandals, and anything else that would set the new generation apart. But in the 1950s, Nader was clearly marching to the beat of a different drummer—ten years ahead of his peers. A Nader classmate at Princeton, Ted Jacobs, recalls: "From the beginning, Nader was unique, a special package, a man with vision coupled with enormous determination."[2]

But that determination did not help him win the "Battle of the Birds" that he waged with *The Daily Princetonian,* a campus newspaper. Nader had noticed that there were dead birds strewn across the campus. He knew that the college groundskeepers routinely sprayed the trees with insecticides that included DDT. And, because the dead birds had not been mutilated, Nader surmised that the DDT must have been killing them. He also knew, firsthand, that students were often accidentally sprayed.

He took one of the dead birds to the editors of *The Daily Princetonian* and explained that the DDT was the most likely cause of the bird deaths. He also questioned the effects the spray might have on humans and suggested that the newspaper look into the matter. The editors laughed at him, saying that some of the nation's brightest chemists and biologists were on the Princeton faculty and that if there were any problems with DDT, these scientists would have already exposed them. Nader was outraged that his fellow students failed to see the potential danger. The newspaper refused even to print a letter-to-the-editor that he wrote calling attention to the situation.

Nader says he learned then that "you can have very smart people around, but if they are not interested in finding out what might be going on . . . things can be missed. It was a perfect example of what people will take for granted if they have been conditioned to trust the system."[3]

Ten years later, in 1962, Rachel Carson wrote her now-famous book *Silent Spring,* in which she correctly claimed that the pesticide DDT posed a huge danger to animals and possibly humans. The chemical had nearly wiped out several bird species. In 1972 the chemical was banned in the United States. Once again, Nader had been ahead of his time. [4]

But in the early 1950s, Dwight Eisenhower was in the White House, and the nation was settling down in the suburbs, buying automobiles and appliances, and raising the "baby boom" generation. Despite the Korean "conflict," the country was—like the Princeton campus—"fat and happy" and content with the status quo.

Thirteen years after his graduation, however, Princeton changed its mind about Ralph Nader's opinions. They gave so much credence to his views that they invited him to teach a course at the university on the American corporation.

During his years at Princeton, he had developed the habit of staying up for most of the night, reading or studying. He also developed a passion for hitchhiking that lasted for many years. He loved the adventure of it and felt that it was a substitute for working in the family restaurant as a way to meet and talk with people from all walks of life, to learn their experiences firsthand. He later said that hitchhiking was one of the greatest educational experiences in the world.

It was hitchhiking and talking with drivers—especially truck drivers—that ignited his lifelong interest in motor-vehicle safety. They told him about accidents they had witnessed or had been involved in. He also saw accidents firsthand over the tens of thousands of miles that he traveled on the nation's highways. He examined crashes closely, noticing the ways in which vehicles were damaged and exactly how people had been injured by being thrown from cars or burned in fires. He began to question the conventional wisdom that blamed all accidents on poor driving, and he wondered whether the way in which vehicles were designed and manufactured might play a role in the safety of drivers and their passengers.

He graduated magna cum laude from Princeton in the spring of 1955 with a major in Oriental Studies. He had applied to Harvard Law School during his last year at Princeton. He had come to believe, as his father did, that a person could do more to help his fellowman by practicing law than by any other means. Surprisingly, Nader's score on the entrance exam was disappointing. But because of his high grades at Princeton, Harvard Law School accepted him. Nevertheless, he insisted on taking the test a second time and raised his score by more than one hundred points. He had to prove that he could do better.

∾∾∾

In the fall of 1955, Nader eagerly set out for Harvard. He was anxious to learn the law and use it to help correct social injustices and protect citizens' rights.

But Nader quickly became disillusioned with Harvard and the kind of law being taught there. "It turned out to be a high-priced tool factory," Nader would later tell people. "But instead of tools, they were producing lawyers who were advocates for the nation's corporations."

This was not what young Nader had expected in a world where he saw growing problems on many fronts: the cities, racial inequality, and the environment. He later complained that Harvard Law School had not presented these issues as challenges to the legal profession, and that law students who worried about concepts of right and wrong, or justice and injustice, were considered "soft" intellectually.

The nation was in the early stages of the civil-rights movement during Nader's Harvard years. The Montgomery (Alabama) bus boycott took place in 1955, the year he entered the law school, and the first Civil Rights Act was passed in 1957. Yet the law school apparently took little notice of these events.

His sister Claire remembers his disappointment: "There was no course on poverty, nothing on landlord/tenant relations, nothing on civil-rights law. There was no law being taught that would make things better for the citizen . . . the kind of law our father envisioned back in Winsted, Connecticut."[5]

Unlike Nader's classmates at Princeton, students at Harvard Law School studied hard and worked long hours. Nader believed they did so because good grades would guarantee them large salaries in the corporate world after graduation. Here again, he went counter-culture.

In protest over the way that Harvard was educating its lawyers, Ralph Nader, the Princeton "grind," decided *not* to study hard. He skipped the classes he found boring or irrelevant, and he took off for days on self-assigned field trips to study legal issues and social problems that were of interest to him even though they were not on the curriculum. One of the unorthodox issues he explored on his own was the design and engineering of automobiles.

Ned Jacobs, Nader's Princeton classmate, was also with him at Harvard. "Ralph paid very little attention to the curriculum," he recalls. "He got through because he was smart."[6]

Throughout his years at Harvard Law School, Nader continued to use hitchhiking as his means of transportation. He also continued to gather information about vehicle safety. Truck drivers reinforced his theories about vehicle fault versus driver fault and told him about injuries that had been caused by poorly built vehicles.

During one hitchhiking trip between Harvard and his Connecticut home, Nader witnessed a brutal automobile accident. As the first person on the scene, he discovered the body of a young girl who had been decapitated by the glove compartment door, which had flown open on impact. Nader never forgot that sight, recalling it when people questioned his motivation in campaigning for auto safety.

Trying to find answers to his questions about how safety features might be designed into automobiles, he visited Harvard's prestigious neighbor, the Massachusetts Institute of Technology (MIT), in search of an engineer who could discuss the safe engineering of automobiles. He found that there was no course taught on auto design or safety engineering.

For Nader, the best thing about his Harvard years was his position on the staff of the *Harvard Law School Record*, the student newspaper. One of the articles he wrote was about the poverty and living conditions of the Native Americans in the Southwest that he had researched during a summer vacation at Princeton. The article was reprinted by an organization in Colorado and sold several hundred copies.

He tackled other subjects, including the exploitation of migrant workers and the myth of black inferiority. In his last year at the law school, he distilled his research on automobile safety into an article entitled, "American Cars: Designed for Death," which was published in the *Record* on December 11, 1958. Several months later, he wrote a similar article, "The Safe Car

Nader speaks at Harvard Law School.

You Can't Buy," which was published in *The Nation* magazine.

Nader graduated from Harvard Law School in 1958, and, armed with his LL.B. degree and a budding free-lance writing career, he was off to . . . the kitchen!

Young men were still drafted into the military in the summer of 1958, and Nader joined the U.S. Army Reserves. Following two months of basic training, the new lawyer was given the job of assistant cook and spent the next four months preparing large quantities of food in an Army kitchen in Fort Dix, New Jersey. He was impressed with the fact that Army food was very wholesome and that everything was made from fresh ingredients: fruits, vegetables, and meat. He liked preparing big pots of soup and baking banana bread for thousands of hungry soldiers.

Following his Army Reserve duty, he was ready to settle down—or was he?

Chapter Three "A one-man lobby for the public"

ᑾᑾᑾIn 1960, Ralph Nader joined the law office of George A. Athanson in Hartford, Connecticut's state capital. He was paid $75 a week to work on auto accident cases, divorces, and wills. But Athanson found that his young associate spent as much time on free legal-aid cases as he did on those that paid fees. Nader recalls that many people came to the office seeking help with problems that they were having with government agencies—problems that amounted to a few hundred dollars. The cases were too small to interest most lawyers, but people came to Nader for help because they thought he would fight for them.

Nader believed that citizens should be able to have ready access to government agencies and services without having to hire lawyers. He became convinced that what was needed in this country was an "ombudsman system" similar to those in Scandinavian countries. An ombudsman is a person who helps ordinary citizens handle problems with the government at all levels. So, in 1961, Nader took off for Europe and, at his own expense, visited Denmark, Sweden, and Finland, interviewing ombudsmen about their work and studying their systems. He returned to the United States, drafted a bill proposing an ombudsman program, and had it introduced into the Connecticut state legislature. The measure failed in his home state, but similar bills, based on his research, were enacted in Hawaii and California.

In addition to his small law practice, Nader taught a few courses at the University of Hartford. But he became restless during the early 1960s. Biographer Kevin Graham calls this Nader's "exploration phase." He traveled around the world, living modestly and writing freelance articles to help defray his expenses. Following his Scandinavian trip, he spent two weeks in the Soviet Union where he interviewed the editors of *Krocodil* magazine, a publication that followed Western culture, and wrote an article for *The Wall Street Journal.*

He spent three months in Latin America in 1963, interviewing hundreds of people and turning out thirty articles for *The Christian Science Monitor* and the *National Observer* on subjects that ranged from economic prospects for Brazil to the meat industry in Uruguay. He traveled to Africa and wrote about the agricultural problems of Ethiopia. Nader's sister Claire says that his travels "stimulated him and allowed him to see the contrasts between the powerful and the poor."[1]

And, he continued to write about automobile safety. *The Nation,* which had published his first article, "The Safe Car You Can't Buy," published an article entitled "Fashion or Safety?" in which Nader criticized the automobile manufacturers for sacrificing vehicle safety in favor of styling. His name was beginning to be associated with automobile safety and design, but he came to feel that he could not make a substantial impact on the issue working from his small Connecticut law office.

∾∾∾

In 1964, Daniel Patrick Moynihan, then assistant secretary of labor for policy planning under President Lyndon B. Johnson (and later a senator from New York), offered Nader a job at the U.S. Department of Labor as a staff consultant on highway safety. Nader had read Moynihan's writing on tire safety, and the two young men had been corresponding for several years.

Nader readily accepted the job and the opportunity it offered to focus full-time on automobile safety. Convinced that the only way to make a difference was through total commitment, he moved to Washington to dedicate himself to that purpose.

For Nader, the job was ideal because it involved researching and writing a report on what role the federal government should take in highway safety. At a time when 50,000 Americans were dying on the nation's highways each year, there were no federal safety standards for automobiles. The report was to make the case for government regulation and provide President Johnson with the ammunition he needed to stand up to the automobile industry.[2] Just as he did back at Princeton, Nader worked eighteen-hour days, seven days a week, often through the night in a deserted office. The final report was several hundred pages long and gave the president the support he needed to prepare legislation setting safety standards for the auto industry. (The legislation, known as the National Traffic and Motor Vehicle Safety Act, was eventually passed by Congress in 1966.) Nader's research on the report, coupled with his own years of study, put him in an excellent position to write a book on the subject. After completing his work on the Labor Department study, he left his consultant post and devoted himself to full-time research and writing.

At the same time, Richard Grossman of Grossman Publishers wanted to publish a book on automobile safety and was looking for someone to write it. He approached James Ridgeway, who had written on the subject for *The New Republic.* Ridgeway knew Ralph Nader and his work and referred Grossman to him. Grossman wanted the book published quickly and set an unusually tight deadline. Once again, Nader put in long days and nights. Working in his room in a boardinghouse near Washington's DuPont Circle, he was able to transform his voluminous research into a manuscript in just four months. Grossman managed to turn the manuscript into a 365-page hardcover book within two months—a process that would normally take a year.

Unsafe at Any Speed was published on November 29, 1965.

"For over half a century the automobile has brought death, injury and the most inestimable sorrow and deprivation to millions of people . . ." the book began. Certainly it was an indictment of the automobile industry, but Nader also set the tone for his future work by criticizing large corporations in general for frequently ignoring the harmful results of the decisions they made. In the case of the automobile, for example, he noted that corporate executives made decisions based on what would make the automobile sell—things like styling, colors, and comfort. There was little, if any, consideration given to features that would make the product safer for the consumer. In Nader's view, the manufacturers sacrificed safety for profit. The book was also critical of the U.S. government for not setting safety standards and passing laws that auto manufacturers had to follow.

Earlier writings on automobile safety tended to hold the driver responsible for the safety of the car. Nader asserted that the design of the car had a direct impact on the safety of those riding in it. No one had previously considered that there could be safety features such as seat belts and shatterproof windshields that could be built into the vehicle and reduce the number of injuries and deaths. Nader wrote:

> The principal reason that the automobile has remained the only transportation vehicle [as opposed to airplanes, trains, and buses] to escape being called to meaningful public account is that the public has never been supplied the information nor offered the quality of competition to enable it to make effective demands through the marketplace and through government for a safe, non-polluting and efficient automobile that can be produced economically. . . . The specialists and researchers outside the industry who could have provided the leadership to stimulate this flow of information by and large chose to remain silent, as did government officials.[3]

The book targeted General Motors' Chevrolet Corvair as a prime example of the industry's negligence. Design flaws, particularly in the rear wheels, caused the car to skid and crash during turns. "The corporate decisions that had produced the Corvair defects," wrote Nader, "were one of the greatest acts of industrial irresponsibility in the present century." He noted that the car was designed to give customers a comfortable and exciting driving experience. But Nader said GM refused to confront the question of the car's safety in order to avoid spoiling its looks and to keep production costs down.

The Corvair had a higher rate of single-car crashes than any other car in its class.[4] GM told owners to take special precautions by keeping the front and rear tires at different pressures, but this correction was hardly foolproof. Since the burden of safety was placed on the driver, GM shrugged off its responsibility and continued to sell the Corvair despite its problems. Using thorough and convincing evidence, Nader accused GM of negligence.[5]

Nader cited other examples of how Detroit regularly sacrificed safety for style and marketing concerns. For example, dashboard indicators—speedometer, gas, and temperature gauges—were often difficult to read, so the driver had to spend time with his eyes off the road looking at the dashboard. The same thing was true of the knobs and switches that controlled windshield wipers, heat, and lights. Such poor design features were common to most vehicles, not just those that were produced by General Motors.

Nader also criticized sharp hood ornaments and tail fins that became dangerous weapons when cars collided with bikers or pedestrians. And he addressed the matter of the "second collision," which is what happens inside the vehicle when people are slammed around after the initial accident. He emphasized that these second collisions were often more deadly than the crash itself and that seat belts or other restraints could prevent serious injury. Nader had never forgotten the sight of the young girl who had been decapitated when she was thrown against an open glove compartment door.

Never before had anyone examined the automotive industry in such a careful, critical way. Prior to *Unsafe at Any Speed,* most people simply assumed that automobiles were as safe as they could possibly be. No one had ever challenged the automobile industry, nor accused the manufacturers of indirect responsibility for thousands of deaths.[6] Nader dedicated his book to Frederick H. Condon, a friend who had been permanently disabled in a car accident.

But Ralph Nader wasn't the only automobile safety show in Washington, D.C., in 1965. While Nader was completing his work for Moynihan and working on his book, Senator Abraham Ribicoff of Connecticut was chairing the Executive Reorganization Subcommittee of the Senate's Government Operations Committee, which was charged with investigating domestic social problems that involved more than one federal agency. Highway safety was a growing social problem. More than 1.5 million Americans had been killed in automobile accidents in the sixty-five years of the automobile's existence. Deaths by traffic accidents had increased by 10 percent between 1963 and 1964 alone, and traffic safety was one of the top six things that Americans said they were worried about that year. The issue of highway traffic safety involved sixteen different federal agencies, so it met the committee's multiple agency requirements.[7]

Senator Ribicoff himself had a history in the area of traffic safety. While Governor of Connecticut, he had focused on two areas of highway safety—getting "drunks and speeders off the roads." He did this through stiff fines and license revocations. But lately, he had become aware of a new book, *Accident Research: Methods and Approaches*, by Dr. William Haddon, E. A. Schman, and D. Klein. It suggested that more attention should be paid to causes other than drinking or speeding as contributors to highway accidents. He became convinced that automobile safety would be a legitimate area for investigation by his new subcommittee even though it meant confronting the Detroit automakers and questioning how they made decisions on matters of automobile safety.[8]

Jerome Sonosky, a young lawyer from Minnesota and the subcommittee's counsel, was charged with putting together the subcommittee staff. He was looking for a "fresh point of view" in the field of automobile safety. A friend suggested that he talk to Ralph Nader. Sonosky recalls scheduling a routine twenty-minute meeting with Nader, but the meeting lasted three hours. "Instead of me sniffing Nader out, he was sniffing me out," recalls Sonosky. "He wasn't about to waste his time if he thought the committee was not going to conduct a serious investigation."[9]

Nader signed on to work with the subcommittee by day and continued to research and write his book at night. He immediately began to fill the minds and files of the staff members with the vast amount of research that he had accumulated over the past decade. His work was the basis of the hearings and helped the committee get off to a fast start. The first set of hearings took place in March 1965, and focused on the federal government's efforts in traffic safety, which Ribicoff said were pitifully small, disorganized, and uncoordinated. In the second set of hearings, held in July, the subcommittee called in automobile industry executives to testify about Detroit's record in auto safety.

∾∾∾

Even before his book was published, Nader was on the radar screen of the automobile industry. Following the subcommittee hearings, his name appeared in letters written by the editor-in-chief of publications at the American Trial Lawyers Association referring lawyers involved in Corvair litigation to Nader, who, he said, had "a substantial amount of information on the Corvair."[10] General Motors wanted to know who this Nader was and where he got the "substantial amount of information on the Corvair."

Nader wrote other articles that were published between the time of the hearings and the November 30 publication of *Unsafe at Any Speed*. A legal reference entitled *American Jurisprudence Proof of Facts* contained a 153-page article by Nader on "Automobile Design Hazards." And the November 1 issue of *The Nation* contained another of his articles—"Profits vs. Engineering—the Corvair Story."

Owners of 1960–1963 Corvairs had already filed more than one hundred lawsuits against General Motors totaling $40 million in damage claims.[11] GM's legal staff felt sure that it could handle the existing suits but believed that Nader's writings—and especially the book—would bolster the bargaining power of those who had sued and touch off a rash of new lawsuits. GM's lawyers also believed that Nader was working with the plaintiffs in these negligence suits in order to turn the Corvair issue into a moneymaking legal proposition for himself. Convinced that he was out to make a fortune at GM's expense, the company's lawyers ordered their investigation of the young lawyer.

Investigators were told: "There's something somewhere [on Nader], find it so they can shut him up."[12] A six-page memo from the head investigator, Vincent Gillen, to his staff summarized the Nader mission: "Our job is to check his life and current activities to determine what makes him tick . . . his politics, his marital status, his friends, his women, his boys . . . drinking, dope, jobs—in all facets of his life."[13]

This was not the first time—nor would it be the last—that people questioned Nader's motives and asked: "What's in it for him?" These questions would follow him throughout his life. And the answers were always disappointing to Nader's critics. GM's investigation in 1965–1966 turned up nothing that would in any way discredit Nader—he had no dark secrets, no bad habits. There was no connection between Nader's work and the Corvair lawsuits, and the young lawyer stood to gain nothing financially from his research into the automobile industry. In fact, he pledged all the royalties from the sale of his book to the cause of auto safety.

Senator Ribicoff was angered by GM's abuse of one of his staff members, and in March 1966 he summoned GM Chairman James Roche to testify before his committee. Following the chairman's admission with an apology that his company had undertaken much more than a routine investigation, Senator Ribicoff addressed Nader: "You and your family can be proud," he noted wryly. "They have put you through the mill, and they haven't found a damn thing wrong with you."[14]

Nader, who also testified at the hearing, was asked for the record by subcommittee member Senator Robert F. Kennedy: "Why are you doing all of this?"

Nader replied:

> If I were trying to prevent cruelty to animals, no one would question my motives. But because I happen to have a scale of priorities that leads me to engage in the prevention of cruelty to humans, my motivations are constantly inquired into. . . .
>
> Basically, my motivation is this: When I see . . . people decapitated, crushed, bloodied, and broken . . . the fatalities and the horrible carnage involved, I ask myself what can the genius of man do to avoid it? And frankly, I think this country and the auto industry are abundantly endowed with the genius to provide an engineering environment for both highway and vehicle that will protect the occupants [of automobiles] from the consequences of their errors. . . .
>
> As I became more and more aware of the tremendous gap between what was possible and what was actual, I became . . . incensed at the way there can be a tremendous amount of injustice and brutality in an industrialized society without any accountability, without any responsibility. People sitting in executive suites can make remote decisions that will someday result in tremendous carnage, but because they are remote in time and space from the consequences of those decisions, there is no accountability.[15]

Nader's work—from his first research as a hitchhiker through his book and his work with Moynihan and the Senate subcommittee—played a key role in the passage

*Nader shakes hands with President Lyndon B. Johnson
after the signing of the 1966 auto and
highway safety acts.*

of the National Traffic and Motor Vehicle Safety Act that President Johnson signed on September 9, 1966. The act established a new federal agency, the National Highway Traffic Safety Administration, which would set safety standards and requirements for auto manufacturers and mandate increased engineering talent and money for improving vehicle safety.

After the act was signed, *The Washington Post* declared: "Most of the credit for making possible this important legislation belongs to one man—Ralph Nader. . . . Through his book, his determination and his seemingly limitless energy, he won. A one-man lobby for the public prevailed over the nation's most powerful industry."[16]

Henry Ford II, chairman of the Ford Motor Company, complained that the new auto safety standards were "unreasonable, arbitrary and technically unfeasible . . . if we can't meet them . . . we'll have to close down." But in 1977 he conceded on the television program *Meet the Press*: "We wouldn't have the kinds of safety built into automobiles that we have unless there had been a federal law."[17]

Over the next several years, Congress would pass regulations that would force manufacturers to incorporate safety features such as seat belts, shoulder harnesses, padded dashboards, collapsible steering columns, more safely designed shift sticks, child seats, and airbags. The Senate hearings taught American consumers a lesson that Ralph Nader had learned as a boy in Winsted, Connecticut: Citizens have the right and the responsibility to speak out against things that are wrong and to call upon their government for protection when necessary.

Even though General Motors had corrected many of its design flaws, Corvair sales declined so drastically—93 percent by some reports—that it was taken off the market within three years. And, finally, GM settled Nader's harassment lawsuit for $425,000. He would eventually use the money to strengthen the fledgling consumer advocacy movement that he had begun and enable him to expose corporate and government wrongdoing for decades to come.

Chapter *Four* "Documenting your intuition"

᷈᷈᷈Nader was pleased that his work had resulted in the passage of major new auto-safety legislation, and he was determined to use the expertise that he had gained to investigate and expose other industry practices that he believed to be unfair or dangerous to the nation's consumers.

The methods he had developed in his case against the auto industry would serve as a blueprint for Nader's future consumer crusades. His first principle: Do the research; get the facts. He called this "documenting your intuition."[1] Working in a small office in the National Press Building or in his Washington boardinghouse room, he read his way through reams of government transcripts, agency reports, congressional testimony, complaints from consumers—whatever information he could obtain to help him identify issues that warranted investigation. (Reading those piles of discarded *Congressional Records* as a teenager in

Connecticut may well have been good preparation for his future campaigns.)

When his research on a particular problem was completed, Nader would issue a comprehensive report, or even publish a book, documenting his findings. He would also write magazine articles based on the investigation, or plant the idea for an article with magazine editors.

With his new national recognition, Nader was able to get the attention of newspaper editors when he issued press releases announcing his latest findings. Frequently, his activities sparked congressional hearings.

Working in this way, he was able to draw the nation's attention to a wide variety of issues: inadequate natural-gas pipeline safety; health hazards in mining operations; unwholesome meat, fish, and poultry processing; avoidable airplane crashes.

The *New Republic* often published Nader's articles. But, despite Nader's new popularity, he never received more than $150 for a *New Republic* story. And some magazines wouldn't consider using an article by Nader. For example, a former assistant editor at *Good Housekeeping* reported that "advertisers would blow their collective tops if they ever saw Nader's name in a *Good Housekeeping* story."[2]

Nader later decided that he could reach more readers more quickly by simply issuing press releases on his findings to newspapers nationwide rather than by relying on magazine articles he had written. His methods worked—he researched, he published, he got the attention of Congress, the media, and the public. "I think of myself as being very practical, because I want to be effective," he has said in talking about how he works. "I want to make changes, and to do that I carefully plan my tactics, and I try to use what power levers I can to get the job done. I am a worker, a plodder."[3]

And Americans were ready to listen, and they were ready for change on many fronts.

༄ ༄ ༄

In the late 1960s and early 1970s, the United States was a country of turbulence and frustration. The Vietnam War was raging. It would be the nation's longest war— 1965 to 1973—and one of its most controversial. Each night millions of Americans watched the war unfold on the evening television news. They saw American soldiers in body bags being loaded onto cargo planes for the trip home; American soldiers lobbing napalm bombs into peasant villages; and children on fire running from their burning homes. These images gave rise to the largest and most successful antiwar movement in the nation's history.

The movement began on American college campuses where many students believed that the U.S. government was killing thousands of people senselessly. In protest, many young men, who had to register for the draft at age eighteen, burned their draft cards. Young women joined the protest. Many of these young people adopted an alternative lifestyle meant to counter what they considered the "establishment"—they grew long hair, dressed in a bohemian way, used drugs, held "love-ins" and antiwar rallies.

At first, the students were dismissed as radicals. But soon, more and more mainstream Americans came to agree with them. The students were making a difference. They had captured the attention of the media and the American people. The movement they had begun would spread from the campuses to the rest of the nation and eventually pressure the government to bring the war to an end.

This period was also a time for social activism. In the South, students and activists were involved in the civil-rights movement, taking part in "sit-ins" and other forms of protest against racial discrimination. Still others were alarmed about the nation's growing environmental problems, and their efforts culminated in massive Earth Day demonstrations in 1970. The women's movement took root in the late 1960s and blossomed in the 1970s.

Several tragic assassinations during these years added to the emotional turmoil. Civil-rights leader Martin Luther King Jr. was shot to death in Memphis, Tennessee, on April 4, 1968. James Earl Ray, a white drifter and escaped convict, was convicted of the murder and received a ninety-nine year sentence. On June 5 of that same year, Senator Robert F. Kennedy, who opposed the Vietnam War and was running for president, was shot and killed just hours after he won the California presidential primary. Sirhan Sirhan, a Palestinian Arab, was arrested at the scene, convicted, and sentenced to life imprisonment, although he claims he had no recollection of where he was or what he did on that night.

All across the country, young people and others were angry and frustrated, and they were eager to transform their anger and frustration into energy for change. Nader's fledgling consumer revolution was challenging the government and the way it responded to the needs of the public. Nader was a frequent speaker on college campuses and sensed the potential power in these young people. It was natural that young activists would gravitate to his cause. Students responded positively to what he called his "gift of outrage" and his passion for creating better, safer lives for Americans. Nader was inundated with résumés of young people seeking employment with him or offering to volunteer.

༄ ༄ ༄

In the summer of 1968, Nader chose seven law-student volunteers as summer interns to be his first student task force. Even though Nader himself had had his differences with Princeton and the Harvard Law School during his own student days, the team he chose was overwhelmingly Ivy League. They were also very unlikely revolutionaries. Among them were: Edward Cox (Princeton, Harvard Law School), the future son-in-law of President Richard M. Nixon; William Taft IV (Yale University, Harvard Law School), the great grandson of President William Howard Taft; and Judy Areen (Cornell University, Yale Law School), whose father was the president of Chrysler Financial Corporation, the automobile manufacturer's financing subsidiary. Although the first team came from Ivy League schools, in subsequent years, many summer interns were chosen from non-Eastern establishment schools.

The first group's mission was to look into the practices of the Federal Trade Commission (FTC), which Nader suspected was not doing enough to protect American consumers from faulty products, fraudulent business practices, and deceptive advertising. The team produced a scathing report on the agency, saying that it was "riddled with people who were placed in their jobs due to patronage or politics, who were time-servers and incompetents, who did little to protect the consumer from anything or anyone."[4] The report documented widespread absenteeism, laziness, alcoholism, and a lack of commitment to the regulatory mission.

The report was greeted with disbelief by Washington officialdom, and President Richard Nixon asked the American Bar Association (ABA) to undertake its own investigation of the FTC. The ABA Commission corroborated the Nader group's findings, saying that the FTC wasted its funds on trivial matters; it characterized the staff as incompetent, especially at the top. The new report said that the agency did less work than it had done ten years earlier and that it should be overhauled or abolished. Bottom line: The distinguished panel of lawyers found exactly the same conditions at the FTC as had Nader's law-school interns. To remedy the situation, President Nixon appointed Caspar Weinberger, then the California state finance director, as the head of the FTC. In one year, Weinberger completely reorganized the agency. He would later serve as Nixon's secretary of Health, Education and Welfare, and President George Bush's secretary of defense.

Inspired by the success of Nader's first student task force and the widespread recognition that its FTC report received, thousands of young law students applied for internships with Nader the following year. He selected about two hundred of the brightest young people, organized them into teams, and charged them with researching the performance of key government agencies and long-ignored social problems.

Nader's task forces were soon turning out explosive reports that made Washington sit up and take notice. *Washington Post* reporter William Grieder dubbed the teams "Nader's Raiders." The tagline stuck. Nader initially disliked the name, believing it trivialized the study groups and sounded like a personality cult. Later

*Nader and his Raiders gather on the steps of the U.S.
Capitol Building in 1969.*

he conceded that the name gave the students' activities a certain style and proved to be a plus for publicity purposes.

The catchy name sounded a lot more glamorous than the actual work. Like their boss, Nader's Raiders worked long hours—nights, holidays, weekends. They read tons of background material and conducted hundreds of interviews for each subject they investigated. Nader never asked the young people to do anything that he himself did not do, but, of course, he expected so much of himself.

Harrison Wellford, an early Nader staffer, believed that the "Raider" tag conjured up the image of a pirate with a swashbuckler mentality. He was quick to disabuse the new interns of this image. "You are not to go into a government agency and prove your worth by rummaging through files that were not open to you, or by seducing a secretary, or by waylaying the department mailman in the halls," Wellford told them. "We play by the rules every step of the way. And there is a very good reason for doing that. In the first place, you can get what you want that way. In the second place, if you don't play by the rules, your credibility is going to be destroyed by personal attack, and the person who destroys it could not have touched it if he had to attack only your facts. Believe me, whenever the investigation begins to hit pay dirt, they will be trying to find ways to discredit you. There is no point in making it easy for them."[5]

Robert Fellmeth, a member of the 1968 FTC task force, also believed the term "Nader's Raiders" was a poor description of what the task forces did. "We are not raiders," he said. "That is a very inaccurate term, with an inaccurate connotation. When you are sitting there at two o'clock in the morning, going over documents page by page by page, thousands and thousands of pages, compiling things, gathering evidence, talking to people, you don't feel like a raider at all. You don't feel like you are on a foray—you feel like a scholar. Whatever it is you are working on, it cannot accurately be called 'raiding.'"[6]

The Raiders saw very little of Nader during the course of a summer. He often said that he wanted people who were self-starters, not people who had to be constantly told what to do. But Nader would ease the way for the interns by calling the agencies or departments that were to be investigated. He would ask for their cooperation and tell them that the students would be calling. And he advised the interns. He told them to "be polite, be persistent, and go prepared. Know your subject. Once the interview starts, go on the offensive and stay there. Don't let the interviewee turn you off or turn you away from what you want, but keep your cool." Nader believed that a successful Raider was a combination of laborious research, good interviewing skills, and moral indignation.[7]

Each of the Raider reports was published as "A Nader Report." In the two-year period between 1969 and 1971, the teams completed thirty reports, among them:

- *The Chemical Feast*—an investigation into the Food and Drug Administration's lax enforcement of food additives

- *The Vanishing Air*—a report on the hazards of air pollution and the way businesses ignored laws designed to stop them from sending deadly chemicals into the air, water, and soil

- *Old Age: The Last Segregation*—an exposé of the indignities and fraud found in homes for the elderly

- *The Interstate Commerce Omission*—an investigation of corruption and incompetence at the Interstate Commerce Commission

- *Bitter Wages: Disease and Injury on the Job*—a report showing how employers ignore dangerous working conditions as well as the suffering of workers injured in the workplace

The first four *Nader Reports* sold more than 450,000 copies. Subsequent teams launched "raids" against the nation's worsening water pollution, *Water Wasteland*; the First National City Bank's conflicts of interest, *Citibank*; the despoliation of land by California land developers, *Politics of Land*; and the degeneration of community mental-health centers, *The Madness Establishment*. By the end of 1972, seventeen books had been published based on the Raiders' investigations.

Applications to join Nader poured in by the thousands, but each year only two hundred or fewer were chosen. Law students complained that it was harder to get on Nader's team than to get into a top law school. The work was intense, and the pay was modest—$150 to $300 per month—but few jobs in Washington were as challenging.

As the summer intern program entered its second year in 1969, Nader decided that he needed both an organizational and physical home for his citizen action activities. He founded the Center for Study of Responsive Law (CSRL, or the Center), a nonprofit consumer action group designed to represent the public against what Nader called "the unholy alliance between corporations and the government."[8] It would be the first of many consumer public-service organizations that Nader would create. The Center's activities and those of the Raiders were carried out in a dilapidated red-brick building on Q Street in northwest Washington. Once an elegant turn-of-the-century mansion, it was said to be in terminal decay by May 1969 when Nader moved in.

The idea for the Center had begun to take shape in Nader's mind back in his college days. He saw a need for a think tank for consumers, a place where consumer-minded lawyers, engineers, and scientists could research, write, and develop policies and strategies. As an offshoot to this core staff, he had envisioned teams of student investigators, which became reality as Nader's Raiders. The Center was funded by grants, private contributions, the fees that Nader received from his speaking engagements, and the books and reports he published.

Within the Center, Nader's core team of lawyers and scientists conducted research and designed tactics that would protect consumers through the enactment of new laws or through investigations that would force changes in the way government agencies such as the Federal Trade Commission functioned. Staff members testified before congressional committees and prepared legislation that supported American consumers.

In the early 1970s, Nader founded several other groups. The first was The Center for Auto Safety, a watchdog group that identified automotive defects and notified the National Highway Traffic Safety Administration (NHTSA), the new agency that Nader's early work had helped create. The Center opened with a backlog of 19,000 auto-safety complaints; 300 new ones arrived each week. It raised money to sustain its operations from the publication of a book, *What To Do With Your Bad Car: An Action Manual for Lemon Owners,* which sold more than 100,000 copies.

In 1971, Nader announced the formation of the Aviation Consumer Action Project (ACAP), another nonprofit group that took on the cause of airline passengers for "better, safer, and less expensive airline service." He was promoting "passenger power" in an ongoing battle with the nation's airlines.[9] As one who traveled tens of thousands of miles every year on airplanes, Nader had firsthand experience with passenger aggravations: late flights, canceled flights, fare increases, bad food. He once told a flight attendant: "The only thing you should be proud to serve on this entire airplane is the little bag of nuts. And you should take the salt off of the nuts."[10]

He filed petitions with the Federal Aviation Administration (FAA) to ban smoking on airlines, which Nader said was both unsafe and unhealthy. He sharply criticized the Civil Aeronautics Board (CAB) for unjustified fare increases, and filed suit to force the release of consumer complaints. To Nader, the FAA and the CAB often behaved as if they were representing the airline industry rather than regulating it.

Nader also set up the Project on Corporate Responsibility, which pushed for a greater voice for consumers and shareholders in shaping corporate policy. One goal was Campaign GM, an effort to make corporate managers and the board more accountable to the entire shareholder base by placing three small shareholders on the GM board of directors.

Still another group, the Corporate Accountability Research Group (CARG), focused on the failure of the government to police corporate monopolies. It explored corporate abuse of power on several fronts: antitrust enforcement, shareholders' rights, environmental pollution, corporate crime, and the need for federal chartering of corporations. This team was headed by Mark Green, author of *The Closed Enterprise System: A Nader Task Force Report on Antitrust Enforcement,* which charged American businesses with bilking consumers out of billions of dollars through price fixing and shoddy merchandise. It called for the breakup of most corporations with assets of $1 billion or more, greater criminal penalties for antitrust violators, a fivefold increase in the size of the government's antitrust force, and an end to political interference in antitrust cases. Mark Green later became New York City's first Public Advocate, the ombudsman for consumers of city services.

The Fishermen's Clean Water Action Project, organized in 1971, sought to recruit the nation's 60 million sports and commercial fishermen into a coalition that would bring pressure on Congress to enact anti–water-pollution bills. Nader pointed out that pollution of the nation's rivers, lakes, and oceans by sewage and industrial waste destroyed the livelihood of commercial fishermen and the recreation of sport fishermen.

Nader would eventually launch fifty such organizations that focused on specific consumer or environmental problems. The investigations, reports, and books that resulted from Nader-related activities got results. According to a 1971 Harris Poll, Nader was the sixth most popular figure in the country. The American people held him in high regard, and the media considered him a leading source of reliable information about consumer issues.

His investigations and reports received widespread press coverage. Often the public would be outraged by what he had uncovered. Frequently, Congress or a federal agency would initiate its own investigation to look into Nader's findings. Between 1966 and 1971, Nader testified before Congress forty times.

Nader's work during those years resulted in a number of significant actions, many of which are still protecting U.S. consumers in the twenty-first century, among them:

- Creation of the National Highway Traffic Safety Administration (NHTSA), which tests automobiles and requires them to have seat belts, padded dashboards, child seats, airbags, shatterproof windshields, and other lifesaving devices

- At least one unsafe automobile—the Corvair—was removed from the market, and automobile recalls—unheard of prior to 1965—have become commonplace

- The 1967 Wholesome Meat Act. This was a major victory for Nader who had been fighting for uniform nationwide regulations, rather than state-by-state regulations.

  This act gave the Department of Agriculture regulatory authority over the meat brokers, dramatically improved the quality of packaged meats, and set limits on the amount of fat in processed meats like hot dogs and bologna.

- The Wholesome Poultry Product Act (1968), which gave the states two years to develop poultry-inspection programs equal to the federal inspection standards

- The Occupational Safety and Health Act (1971), resulting in the creation of the Occupational Safety and Health Administration (OSHA), which oversees the safety of Americans in the workplace

- The Environmental Protection Agency (EPA) created in 1970 to protect the nation's environment. It brought the functions of fifteen federal programs dealing with pollution under single management.

- Consumer Product Safety Commission, an independent agency of the U.S. government created in l972 to protect consumers from unsafe products that can cause illness, injury, or death

- The Freedom of Information Act (1974), which gave the public access to all information held by the government except in matters of national security

- The Radiation Control Act (1968), which placed limits on the radiation emissions from television sets and X-rays

- The Coal Mine Health and Safety Act (1969), which set guidelines for eliminating hazardous working conditions in coal mines

Of course, Nader and his organizations did not accomplish all these actions single-handedly. Other groups were often involved as well. For instance, Consumers Union (CU), an organization dedicated to providing information to consumers on products and services and educating the public, had been in operation since 1936. Its laboratories were testing grounds for consumer products, including the automobile, and the results of the tests were released to the public through its publication, *Consumer Reports*. Nader served on CU's board from 1967 to 1973. During his tenure, the organization helped establish the National Commission on Product Safety and set up consumer advocacy offices in Washington, D.C., San Francisco, California, and Austin, Texas.

Not all Nader studies resulted in immediate legislation but played key roles in future laws and regulatory initiatives. In just those few years, Nader had taken a giant step toward changing the way Americans looked at the products they bought and the corporations that manufactured them. He had also begun to scrutinize the government agencies that had been created to protect the health and welfare of the American public.

It was a good beginning.

Chapter Five "Laboratories of Democracy"

∞∞∞Nader was a whirlwind of activity in the early 1970s. He was creating new advocacy groups, training new leaders, conducting even more investigations, and publishing the findings. But his true goal was not simply to expand his own operations; it was also to transform American consumers into active, informed, questioning individuals, and to convince them that they could—and should—play a crucial role in making business and government accountable to them. He wanted the American people to realize that they had immense power if only they chose to use it.

Nader took a giant step toward achieving that outcome in 1971 when he founded the Public Interest Research Group (PIRG), a law firm that would have public-interest issues as clients rather than people or corporations. The idea for such an organization had been in his mind since law school, where he observed that courageous lawyers always represented the defense. They defended unpopular causes, people who were wrongfully accused, and minority groups. He wanted that same kind of courageous lawyer to go on the offense, to take the lead in forcing the institutions of society to be more responsive to the needs of the people.

He staffed the PIRG with twelve lawyers and a medical doctor, each with a different area of expertise. He was able to provide start-up funds for the new group with money he received from General Motors in settlement of the harassment and invasion of privacy lawsuit that he had filed against the company. Ironically, GM trucks would be a target for PIRG lawyers within a year of the organization's launch.

PIRG lawyers were paid $4,500 per year at a time when lawyers entering other Washington law firms were paid four times that amount. Like all Nader-run enterprises—and like the man himself—PIRG was a very frugal operation. Nader was very careful about how he spent the contributions, grants, and donations that supported his organizations.

Early in PIRG's history, Nader wanted to recruit law professors to work with him during their sabbaticals, which are periods of several months or a year spent studying or traveling instead of teaching. Here is how he described his operation in a notice sent to law schools:

> *Attention: Sabbatical-bound Professors.*
> *Ralph Nader is seeking law-school faculty members to work with his Public Interest Research Group in Washington, D.C. The pay is minimal, the work voluminous, the office décor early Salvation Army.*
>
> *The compensation: Nader is at the cutting edge of a not-so-quiet legal revolution.*

Working with the Public Interest Group pro-
vides the opportunity to make a substantial
contribution to the growth and stature of
public-interest law . . . in the "rejuvenating"
atmosphere of Washington, D.C.[1]

Nader referred to the PIRG law firm as his action arm. Lawyers signed on for one year, and even though many stayed longer, Nader always preferred that the Washington-based PIRG stay small and have a high turnover. He wanted those young lawyers to leave PIRG and put their public-interest experience to work in other law firms or corporations.

The first team of PIRG lawyers set to work on consumer issues within the Washington bureaucracy and beyond. Two of them petitioned the Food and Drug Administration (FDA) to require disclosures of the phosphate content of laundry detergents. Another filed a lawsuit to make the FDA require better health warnings on birth-control pills. Two of them moved to West Virginia to oppose Union Carbide Corporation plants that they believed were polluting nearby communities. The lawyers mobilized the local citizenry, and with Nader generating the publicity, forced Union Carbide into speeding up its pollution-control campaign.[2]

Still others worked on banking, tax reform, and health issues. Frequently they had to sue the government in order to get federal agencies to release information, as they were required to do under the 1966 Freedom of Information Act (FOIA). PIRG lawyers led the movement to have General Motors recall 500,000 trucks with faulty tire rims. They became involved with the issues of excessive corporate tax write-offs, which Nader called a form of corporate welfare, and deceptive advertising for Excedrin pain medication. They participated in Civil Service hearings for fired federal employees and wrote the guidelines for the Fair Credit Reporting Act, which set regulations to ensure accuracy and fairness in credit reporting by consumer reporting agencies. PIRG took on the Federal National Mortgage Association (known as "Fannie Mae") on the issue of mortgage-lending forms, which PIRG said were weighted in favor of the lender over the borrower.

ᘉᘉᘉ

The Washington PIRG team was a success, but Nader wasn't satisfied. He wanted to see the PIRG concept bloom on the national level, taking root in towns and cities across the United States. To meet that goal, two of the original Washington PIRG lawyers focused on organizing students on college campuses. With Nader's help—he spoke on more than one hundred college campuses every year—they created a student-led PIRG movement that continues to thrive as a citizen-action force today.

The student PIRG concept first became a reality on the University of Oregon campus following one of Nader's speeches in which he launched that idea. The idea gained support, and soon all seven schools in the state college system approved the establishment of the Oregon Student Public Interest Research Group, known as OSPIRG. It next took hold in Minnesota where a single graduate student organized a statewide movement of more than 50,000 students.

Each student group was financed and run by students, but guided by a small professional staff. Nader and Donald Ross, an original member of the first PIRG law firm in Washington, wrote a book called *Action for Change*, which outlined everything a group needed to know about starting and operating a Public Interest

Research Group. Soon students across the country were reading this "how-to" manual and becoming citizen activists, selecting local issues and applying the PIRG action plan.

In New Hampshire, a student-led PIRG helped lead the battle against a planned $600 million oil refinery that was opposed by the residents of two towns but had the support of the governor. The project failed, due primarily to the organizing efforts of the state's PIRG and the pressure placed on members of the New Hampshire legislature.

MASSPIRG, in Massachusetts, placed an initiative on the state's ballot aimed at reducing the use of toxic chemicals statewide. Voters approved the measure by the largest margin of any initiative in the state's history. Similar efforts by PIRGs in Oregon and Washington convinced state legislators and chemical industry officials to negotiate laws for reducing the use of toxic chemicals. In Maine, PIRG sued oil companies for harming the environment. Elsewhere, PIRGs tackled recycling, pollution, sex discrimination, energy, and public health and safety issues.

"PIRGs have given people a taste of citizen action," Nader said. "I call them 'laboratories of democracy,' because they show people what can be done and then give them tools they can use throughout their lives."[3] Nader did not see the nationwide expansion of the PIRGs as a way to acquire power for himself or his organization. Rather, he viewed the growth as a way to disperse power and put it into the hands of the citizens.

ᘓᘓᘓ

Meanwhile, in Washington, D.C., Nader and his teams were having an impact on the way corporations did business. "In the pre-Nader era, the Washington lawyers performed efficiently and expensively for their corporate clients, but with Nader to contend with, their jobs were a lot more difficult," wrote Nader biographer Robert Buckhorn in 1972. "Nader and his fellow consumerists and environmentalists made it harder for the lawyers to work their legal magic on the government. . . ."[4]

Nader had been a witness to the "legal magic worked on government." These were the deals made between the lawyers and lobbyists for giant corporations and the federal agencies that were supposed to be regulating them. He believed that if consumers had their legal representatives roaming the agencies and Congress, the playing field would be more level. Nader wanted the public to know how the corporate lawyers often exercised their power to the detriment of consumers, and about a system in which former executives of the corporations being regulated often headed the regulatory agencies.

Nader believed that this arrangement, known as the "old boy network," resulted in weakened consumer protections. He felt that collaboration between agency heads and corporate lawyers that were of like mind produced the kinds of deals that watered down warning labels on cigarettes, postponed the deadline for mandatory air bags in automobiles, and allowed automakers to deliberately keep antipollution devices off the market.

At one point, Nader said that 10,000 lawyers were needed in Washington to work for the public interest in order to counter the 15,000 (1971 figure) lobbyists who represented America's corporations and other powerful institutions. Nader contended: "It's not too much to ask that the system make room for a people's lobby."[5]

In fact, that is what he eventually did ask. Nader had met Joan Claybrook in 1966 when she was a congressional aide to Representative James Mackay, a Democrat from Georgia. MacKay was interested in auto safety and asked Claybrook to set up an appointment with Nader. Nader and Claybrook have been close, both personally and professionally, ever since. She suggested that he form a lobbying group that would be different from those that undertook investigations, wrote legislation, and filed lawsuits. It would be a federation of advocacy groups active in many different forums: Congress, federal agencies, the courts, the news media, and in selected congressional districts. It would be called "Public Citizen" and would be the eyes, ears, and voice of American consumers in Washington. Claybrook, who was then working at the National Highway Traffic Safety Administration, went to work for Nader in 1970.

Together they launched Public Citizen in 1971 with two mass mailings that attracted more than 62,000 members and donations totaling more than $1 million. This enthusiastic support for Nader's latest endeavor was an indication of the esteem in which the country held Ralph Nader in the early 1970s.

Two of the first groups to come under the Public Citizen umbrella were the Health Research Group and the Litigation Group. The Health Research Group (HRG) was headed by Sidney M. Wolfe, M.D., a researcher at the National Institutes of Health, who had worked with Nader earlier in a recall of millions of bottles of bacteria-contaminated intravenous fluid, which had infected 150 people and killed nine. He and Nader agreed that a special watchdog group was needed for the health field. The HRG's first project was a petition to the FDA requesting a ban on Red Dye No. 2, a popular, but nutritionally worthless, dye used to enhance the color appeal of food. HRG believed the dye could cause

Nader joins Joan Claybrook, then president of Public Citizen, in a 1989 press conference relating to concerns over skyrocketing auto insurance rates.

cancer. The campaign attracted widespread public attention and alerted consumers to the frequent use of potentially hazardous additives to the nation's food supply. It was a five-year battle, but HRG prevailed and the FDA banned the dye.

The second Public Citizen group, the Litigation Group, was headed by Alan B. Morrison, an assistant U.S. attorney in the Southern District of New York City. Morrison and Nader met in 1971 through a law student who had been one of Nader's summer interns. In 1972 they joined forces to found the Litigation Group, one of the few public-interest law firms in Washington, D.C. They focused on "representing the unrepresented"[6] and their clients included consumers who were harmed by cancer-causing food additives, workers exposed to toxic substances on the job, union members deprived of their rights by labor unions, and citizens victimized by the legal profession's price-fixing. Most of the cases they pursued were "class action" in nature because they advanced a new legal principle on behalf of victims in similar situations.

Two years later, Nader launched Congress Watch, an outgrowth of an earlier, monumental effort called the Congress Project, which had investigated the record of every member of the U.S. Senate and House of Representatives.

Congress Watch did just what its name implied. It watched congressional activities and lobbied on behalf of consumer and citizen interests in areas such as health, safety, and the environment. It championed the causes of the people against the power of large corporations, demanding an end to "corporate welfare," which Nader identified as "the enormous number of subsidies, bailouts, giveaways, tax loopholes, debt revocations, loan guarantees, discounted insurance, and other benefits conferred by government on business."[7]

Congress Watch fought to preserve citizen access to the courts in confronting alleged corporate wrongdoing, and it sought to strengthen democracy by exposing the harmful impact of money in politics. Thirty years before it became a major presidential campaign issue, Public Citizen was lobbying for campaign-finance reform.

Eventually Public Citizen would encompass six divisions, headquartered in Washington. Each had its own director, policy apparatus, and public identity. But they all shared Public Citizen's central administrative and fund-raising system headed by Joan Claybrook.

∾∾∾

One of Nader's earliest and ongoing battles was over access to information. This should not have been an issue. The Freedom of Information Act (FOIA), passed by Congress in 1966, gave the public access to all information held by the government except in matters of national security. Anyone, not just consumer-advocacy groups like Nader's or investigative reporters, had a right to ask for and receive any document from anywhere within the federal government. The first Nader's Raiders investigation of the Federal Trade Commission unearthed most of its information by threatening to sue the agency under the FOIA. Later, Nader's PIRG lawyers filed numerous suits against the government in order to obtain documents.

The law was in place, but by the early 1970s corporations and government agencies had learned how to stall inquiries and limit the amount of information they made public. Nader became frustrated with the weakening of the FOIA and, under the Public Citizen tent, he set up the Freedom of Information Clearing House to help both individuals and organizations use the FOIA more effectively. "Secrecy ruins democracy," he warned, "and information supports it. If you don't know and can't find out, you can't do anything." [8]

In 1974, Senator Edward Kennedy (Democrat of Massachusetts) led the Senate effort to pass a much tougher version of the FOIA. New amendments made it a more responsive instrument, and federal agencies had to respond to requests for information within two weeks. And those who successfully sued government

Nader and Senator Edward M. Kennedy (D-Mass.) chat after the Senate FOIA subcommittee hearings in which Nader proposed a public counsel corporation.

agencies in order to get information were allowed to recover their legal fees. "The changes really made the act work," says Nader. "It gave it a lot more teeth and the ability to do good."[9]

Thanks to the tougher FOIA, groups like Nader's, as well as investigative newspaper and television reporters, have been able to expose thousands of cases of government waste, mistakes, and wrongdoing. They have uncovered dangerous products, environmental hazards, unhealthy foods, and inferior medical care. Public Citizen used information gathered using the FOIA to reveal collusion between a drug company and the government to hide information about a drug that was responsible for the deaths of fifty elderly patients. Company officials were eventually charged with crimes and prosecuted.

∾∾∾

There was one more major battle for Ralph Nader to wage in the 1970s—the one against nuclear power, which he called "our technological Vietnam." He became skeptical about nuclear power as early as 1970 when he had attended a conference at the Oak Ridge National Laboratory—a once-secret Atomic Energy Commission (AEC) operation that developed the uranium and plutonium used in the atomic bomb. He found that the nuclear engineers at the presentation would not or could not answer questions such as, "What would happen if a nuclear system goes wrong?"

Later Nader's skepticism turned to outright opposition when he read an AEC-funded study by two scientists who estimated that 16,000 more Americans would contract cancer or leukemia every year if the U.S. population were exposed to the doses of radiation emissions from nuclear-power plants that were permissible at that time.[10] At Nader's request, Senator Edmund Muskie (Democrat from Maine) held the country's first official inquiry into the safety of nuclear power.

At that time, the government expected to have a thousand nuclear plants on-line in the United States by the year 2000, with a hundred of them in California alone. With twenty-three plants already built and seventy more on order, the nuclear-power industry had momentum on its side and thought they could not be stopped. They told *The New York Times* that "Nader is too late on this one. He can't stop us."

"Of course that's all I had to hear," was Nader's comment.[11]

He worried about the operational safety of the nuclear plants. He was also concerned about the disposal of the radioactive waste produced by the plants. Where would it be sent? How would it be stored? The industry and the AEC, later named the Nuclear Regulatory Commission (NRC), had few answers. Then there was the cost of the nuclear plants; they were expensive to build and to operate, and Nader found that closing a plant could cost as much as building it because of the radioactive wastes involved.

In 1972, antinuclear groups such as Friends of the Earth and the Union of Concerned Scientists pressured the AEC to hold hearings on nuclear plant safety. The sessions revealed numerous industry failures in the area of plant safety. More important, the inquiry group also discovered that the AEC had been trying to cover up those failures.

Citizen opposition to nuclear power was growing, but there was no national focus. Nader and Claybrook, once again operating under the aegis of Public Citizen, created the Critical Mass Energy Project and organized Critical Mass '74. This was the first national antinuclear gathering. In scientific terms, "critical mass" refers to the amount of radioactive material needed to sustain a chain reaction at a constant rate. But Nader used "critical mass"[12] to mean the joining together of people and organizations in large enough numbers to stop nuclear power.

Twelve hundred antinuclear activists attended the weekend conference, which served as both a training session and a means of unifying the diverse groups. The participants met experts in the nuclear-power field and were briefed on citizen-action tactics. They began to see themselves as part of a larger movement and took home instruction manuals containing the information they needed to put the safe-energy movement into action. A second conference was held the following year, in 1975.

Public Citizen's Critical Mass Energy Project continued to support the antinuclear groups financially and armed them with research and reports that documented the many problems associated with nuclear energy. Several "anti-nuke" rallies (as they came to be called) attracted hundreds of thousands of supporters in New York City and Washington, D.C. Those events drew heavy media attention and forced the nation to take a hard look at the issue. Public support for nuclear-power plants dwindled, as did the demands of utility companies for new reactors. No new plants have been built since 1978. (In 2001, President George W. Bush proposed the expansion of nuclear generation as part of its energy program.)

Once again Nader and company had made a major impact. The nuclear-power industry had underestimated what citizen advocates could accomplish.

The nuclear industry was dealt another blow on March 28, 1979, when a failure of the cooling system of a nuclear reactor in a power plant at Three Mile Island in Pennsylvania led to partial melting of its uranium core and the production of hydrogen gas. This raised fears of explosion and dispersal of radioactivity. Thousands living near the plant were evacuated before the twelve-day crisis ended. Some radioactive water and gases were released. A federal investigation assigned blame to human, mechanical, and design errors. It recommended changes in reactor licensing and personnel training, as well as in the structure and function of the NRC itself. The accident further increased public concern over the dangers of nuclear power.

Seven years later, a disaster occurred at a nuclear-power plant in Chernobyl, in what was then the Soviet Union. Explosions and fire spread radioactive material over thousands of miles, killing thousands of people and injuring millions more. In 1999, another, less serious, accident occurred in Tokaimura, Japan, when an employee made a mistake that caused an explosion involving nuclear materials.

Critical Mass, with the help of the legal arm of Public Citizen, has continued to monitor the nuclear-power industry. The group has led the battle against an NRC proposal to allow low-level radioactive waste to be dumped in the normal waste stream—landfills, incinerators, and recycled products. By deregulating those wastes, calling them Below Regulatory Concern (or BRC), the agency hoped to ignore 30 percent of the low-level wastes generated by nuclear-power plants. Had this been allowed, the dumping would have continued almost entirely without oversight or enforcement. Since the NRC first proposed this lax BRC policy, Critical Mass has successfully countered it at every opportunity, in courts and before Congress.[13]

Chapter Six "We've resurrected Ralph Nader"

∾∾∾It had been a breathtaking ten years—from the 1965 publication of *Unsafe at Any Speed* to the antinuclear movement. There had been hundreds of investigations and exposés; thirty-five books; dozens of consumer-action groups; new laws and tighter regulations; and a growing public awareness of citizen empowerment.

The health and safety of the people of the United States were protected by new agencies and laws that owed their existence directly or indirectly to Ralph Nader—the National Highway Traffic Safety Administration (NHTSA), the Environmental Protection Agency (EPA), the Consumer Product Safety Commission (CPSC), and the Occupational Safety and Health Administration (OSHA).

In 1974 a *U.S. News & World Report* national survey showed Nader to be the fourth most influential person in the United States. His picture was on the cover, together with those of President Richard Nixon and

Secretary of State Henry Kissinger, under a headline that asked: "Who Runs America?" The magazine reported: "Mr. Nader came through in survey comments as a man you can trust."

Clearly Ralph Nader was at the top of his game. But something happened; Nader soon lost influence.

When Jimmy Carter became president in 1977, some of Nader's protégés were recruited for positions in his administration. That may have slowed Nader's operation somewhat, but it could not explain his abrupt disappearance from the national stage. Many theories have been advanced to explain Nader's sudden loss of influence at the end of the 1970s and into the 1980s, among them:

- Corporations were fighting back. Nader had embarrassed them, made them admit wrongdoing, and forced them to treat consumers more fairly. Now they unleashed their money and power in an all-out effort to regain their influence over government decision-making. Their lobbyists painted Nader as a man who had gone too far and asked too much.

- People were tired of activism of all kinds. The Vietnam War had ended, the Environmental Protection Agency and other consumer safeguards were in place, and the Civil Rights Acts of 1964, 1965, and 1968 had been passed. The public felt that the government, through the newly created laws and agencies, was now doing the job of protecting the nation's health and safety.

- There was a public backlash against Nader's sustained attacks on the American corporate structure. As the 1970s ended, the economy was declining, inflation rates were high, there was an energy shortage, unemployment was on the rise, and people were afraid of losing their jobs.

- Even though Jimmy Carter, a Democrat, was elected president in 1976, the electorate was turning more conservative and elected a Republican majority to Congress in 1978. Republicans are traditionally more probusiness and antiregulation than are Democrats.

- The fact that Nader had enjoyed such success with the media and received such widespread press coverage for so many years eventually worked against him. The "media darling" was no longer new and, therefore, no longer newsworthy. Also, the media came to resent Nader's desire for privacy—and he was intensely private. He saw no need to talk to reporters about where he lived, how he lived, how he spent his time or his money. He had never married, because he believed his 24/7 work schedule would be unfair to a family. He was neither on the Washington social circuit nor seen "on the town." The press, which was relying more and more on personality stories, found that Nader's lifestyle was not "good copy."

- People were uncomfortable with his constant criticism of corporate America, and an increasingly conservative public considered his zealous campaigns to be anticapitalist.

- He was too hard-hitting. Because he always spoke his mind, some people thought that he was too brash, too forceful. He did not compromise, and eventually even his supporters—including those in Congress—grew tired of what they perceived to be his "all-or-nothing" attitude.

- Nader and Public Citizen had fought hard for the establishment of a consumer-protection agency, which would represent consumer interests as they came before the government's various agencies. Corporations fought just as hard against the proposed agency, and in 1978 it was narrowly defeated in the U.S. House of Representatives. Also that year, automakers succeeded in squelching Nader's efforts to impose mandatory inflatable air bags in automobiles. After so many successes, Nader was beginning to lose battles.

- Finally, with the election of Republican Ronald Reagan (former governor of California) as president in 1980, Nader's causes became old news—the opposite of what then became popular in Washington. Reagan had campaigned on a promise to "get the government off people's backs," and his "free market" philosophy took the teeth out of agencies that had previously guarded the public interest. Funding cuts gutted regulatory agencies, and those appointed by Reagan to run them were often pro-corporation rather than advocates for consumers.

It is likely that the explanation of why Nader and his organizations no longer made headlines includes some or all of the above.

Nader continued to work hard on the issues. "But," he recalls, "suddenly all we could do was play defense. And once you're on the defensive—trying to protect what already exists—it's hard to switch to offense. They were terrible times."[1] He acknowledges that by the end of the 1970s and into the 1980s the corporations were fighting back. "We had done our job too well," he says.

"Now they had their armies of lobbyists all over Washington."[2]

Still, the reason he all but disappeared from the headlines and the nightly television news was, simply, that the press stopped covering him. "We were on to the Savings and Loan (S&L) crisis long before any reports came out in the *Wall Street Journal* or *The New York Times*," Nader says. "We held press conferences to announce our findings and no one covered them."[3] The crisis involved a category of banks called savings-and-loan associations, which were deregulated in the 1980s. They attracted depositors by offering higher-than-average interest rates and often invested the money in risky deals. When those deals went bad, the S&Ls collapsed, threatening the nation's financial stability. Eventually Congress came to the aid of the industry with a $500 billion bailout—paid for by American taxpayers.

"That was a lot of wasted money that could have paid for a lot of health care," Nader says looking back. "Perhaps a certain amount of regulation isn't such a bad idea," he now says wryly.[4]

Why wasn't the press covering Nader? He suggests several reasons. "First," he says, "the corporations, with all their advertising revenue in hand, met with editors and made it clear that they didn't like what we were doing. . . ." Nader maintains that *The New York Times*, in particular, was instrumental in stopping the coverage of consumer-advocacy activities in Washington. "When Rosenthal [A.M. Rosenthal] took over as [managing] editor of *The New York Times* in 1972, he told reporters in the Washington bureau to stop covering us," Nader says. "He was starting supplement sections in Long Island and Westchester County [suburbs of New York City] and he needed a lot more advertisers.

"I wrote Rosenthal about the situation," Nader continues. "His reply was, basically, that there was no problem. But there was a problem. We were being closed out. And once *The New York Times* closes you out, *The Washington Post* follows suit, because the two are big competitors. And the television networks feed off the *Times* and the *Post*, so if your story isn't in those morning papers, it doesn't appear on the evening television news."[5]

"Second," Nader maintains, "the press was in a general state of decay with more attention being paid to lifestyle rather than hard news. They were looking for more O.J. Simpson [the ex-football player accused of murdering his wife] and Tanya Harding [the figure skater who bashed the knee of a competitor] and that kind of thing. One way to get into the press is to misbehave personally," he says. "That's not the way we operate, so the press didn't have any gossip to deal with. The media itself was moving more and more into fluff, sensationalism, sex, addictions, and celebrities."[6]

He notes, too, that the media had become a part of corporate conglomerates. "Look at who owns them," he says. Citing General Electric's ownership of NBC (the National Broadcasting Company), he adds, "the media has the same interests as the corporations we were exposing."[7]

Another reason Nader believes his activities received less coverage is that he had succeeded too well. "We demonstrated that people were very interested in consumer issues, and the stories we generated attracted viewers and readers. Before us, there were no consumer reporters, no consumer beats, very little investigative reporting." Nader's efforts to strengthen the Freedom of Information Act (FOIA) gave reporters the tools they needed to get consumer stories. "Now," he says, "they can get the stories themselves, but they can only go so far because of advertisers and because of who owns them. It's a subtle form of self-censorship."[8]

Still, despite the absence of media attention and influence during the 1980s, Nader remained active, continuing to nurture the web of Washington-based organizations he had launched a decade earlier. But many believed that his days on the public stage were over.

ᘯᘯᘯ

Those were hard years for Nader personally, as well. In April 1986 he developed Bell's palsy, a disease that paralyzed the left side of his face, making it hard for him to talk, eat, or smile. His eyelid drooped, and he wore dark glasses to conceal the condition. Gradually he recovered, but his case had been severe, and he still experiences some residual effects of the disease.

Later that year, in August, his older and much-loved brother, Shafeek, died of prostate cancer. He had been a great advocate of community colleges, and established one in Winsted. He then worked with communities throughout the country helping them establish local two-year colleges. The two brothers had shared a special bond. "Shaf was a great older brother," says Claire Nader. "He had a fine hand in helping all of us, and he was a great influence on Ralph. The first child of an immigrant family is always like a bridge between the old world and the new, between parents and younger siblings."[9] Nader says that losing his brother was one of the hardest things he has ever faced.

Several Nader biographers have written that the sadness and disappointments of the 1980s—professional and personal—left him depressed and withdrawn. But Nader says he emerged from this period energized. "I'm like a doctor," he says, "I see problems every day, all day. I don't get depressed."[10]

Nader had maintained close ties with his hometown of Winsted, Connecticut, where he often joined family members in local civic-action projects. Following his brother's death, Nader returned to Winsted and assisted the family in setting up the Shafeek Nader Trust, which established the office of Community Attorney for Winsted. The full-time lawyer is an advocate for the townspeople, paid by the Trust, and oversees issues that range from health care to the water system to taxation. As "citizen watchdog," the Community Attorney helps the townspeople deal with governmental agencies and legal authorities in much the same way Nader had proposed in his ombudsman plan back in 1961.

∾∾∾

As the "terrible times" of the 1980s drew to a close, Nader seemed intent on recapturing the nation's attention. Revitalized, he mounted two ambitious crusades: one against the California insurance industry and the other against the U.S. Congress. Ralph Nader was out of the shadows.

In 1988 there was a battle in California over insurance rates, which had been rising steadily, unchecked, for many years. Consumers felt they were paying more than they could afford and placed a referendum to get rates lowered on the ballot. It was known as Proposition 103, and Nader strongly supported it.

He went to work in California with the same vigor and expertise that he had shown in his battles of the 1960s and 1970s. The insurance companies fought Proposition 103 with all the manpower and money at their disposal. In the end, they had spent $70 million.

The Nader family established the Community Attorney office in an old factory building in downtown Winsted, Connecticut.

The backers of the proposition had only $2 million to spend. But they had Ralph Nader. His name had been out of the headlines, but it still carried weight with the public. A poll taken at the time showed that 67 percent of voters said they would vote for any measure if Ralph Nader supported it. Posters supporting the referendum simply said, "Nader 103." That was enough for the voters. Proposition 103 passed and forced the insurance companies into an unprecedented rate rollback. In addition, it put a curb on future increases.

A story circulated at the time about two insurance executives who were reflecting on the lost battle. Said one: " I can't believe this. We are down $70 million. And, we've resurrected Ralph Nader!"[11]

Back in Washington, Nader led the fight against a proposed 51 percent congressional pay raise. He took to the radio talk-show circuit to publicize and oppose the

During a 1977 press conference on auto safety, Nader
watches an air bag simulator demonstration.

issue. Most members of Congress grew uneasy with
Nader's spotlight on the pay increase and voted against
it—at least for that year.

He was more visible and seemed to be presenting
consumer issues with a bit more flare. In 1988 celebrities Dustin Hoffman, Paul Newman, and Phil Donahue

joined him in publicly demonstrating the safety benefits of the inflate-on-impact automobile air bag. Soon
after, manufacturers announced that the device would
be standard in some models.

As the last decade of the twentieth century rolled
out, Nader was still writing (*Winning the Insurance
Game* was published in 1990) and still overseeing the
consumer-advocacy groups he had founded (there
were more than fifty), but focusing primarily on his
firstborn, the Center for Study of Responsive Law, and
the Corporate Accountability Research Group.

Yet even though he had somewhat more visibility in
the 1990s, the national press was still not reporting
about him or about the issues of democracy to which
he had devoted his life. But he had not lost hope.
"Sometimes you just have to say, 'OK, it didn't work out
this way, we'll have to find another way to prevail'," he
says.

Chapter Seven   "... Unlike any other candidate"

∾∾∾In 1976, Nader supporters in Massachusetts had placed his name on the ballot as a presidential candidate, but he demanded that it be removed. For years he had insisted that he would never run for office. But by 1992, he was beginning to rethink his position.

"In the early days it was the corporations that were blocking citizen action, so we could turn to the political system for redress," he said. "We won laws and regulations that saved lives. But now the political system was locking arms with the corporate system and that blocked civic action. At that point," he concludes, "you have two choices. One is you go into politics, or two, you retire to Monterey [California] and watch the whales."[1]

The whales would have to wait. Nader's choice was to enter politics, but he proceeded at a very modest pace.

In 1991, Nader was a write-in candidate in the New Hampshire presidential primary. He received 2 percent each of the Democratic and Republican vote. This was

Candidate Nader campaigns during the 1991
New Hampshire primary.

considered a fairly impressive showing since he had spent no money. He was just testing the water, but he found that he enjoyed campaigning as a way to reach people.

In 1996, a group of prominent members of California's Green Party (Greens) asked Nader if he would enter their state's presidential primary. The Green Party in the United States began in 1984, and by 1996 had just 80,000 members in only twenty-five states. Its platform supports nonviolence, social justice, environmentalism, respect for diversity, global

*During the 1996 presidential campaign,
Nader speaks to a crowd at UCLA.*

responsibility, and community-based economics and democracy.[2]

Nader was comfortable with the Greens and saw merit in energizing and strengthening the party so that it could become an alternative to the two major U.S.

parties. "I wanted to help inspire a new generation of activists—people who wanted to change politics," he says.[3]

He agreed to run as a Green but on his own terms: He did no fund-raising, accepted no campaign contributions, and aired no television commercials. Instead, he gave scores of speeches and interviews and published position papers on the Internet, while the Greens tried to organize activities at the state level and run the day-to-day operations of the campaign. The effort was hardly an all-out presidential campaign—Nader's name was on the ballot in fewer than half of the states, and he spent less than $5,000. He received slightly fewer than 700,000 votes.

Four years later, however, Nader was ready for a serious nationwide effort. "My candidacy had been evolving," Nader says. "There was no sudden decision, no one thing that pushed me over the edge in 2000."[4] He was, however, frustrated by what he considered to be the "Republicanization" of the Democratic Party and President Clinton's drift to the right. "He wouldn't even support studies in his own Department of Transportation that would have kept the speed limit at 55," Nader says. "Thousands of people have been killed and injured needlessly since the limit was increased. Plus, it means more air pollution, more imported oil, and billions of dollars in medical costs.

"In 1992, Clinton had promised that by the year 2000 the fuel efficiency of vehicles would be 40 miles (64 kilometers) per gallon," Nader continues. "Instead he presided over a decline in mileage—it dropped to 24.5. He was going to curb the fat cats and get campaign reform passed. There had been one broken promise after another."[5] Nader admits now that he "should have made a serious run for president back in 1992, but that's in retrospect."[6] And he doesn't like to look back.

On February 21, 2000, in Washington, D.C., Nader announced his candidacy for the Green Party's nomination for president. He opened his statement by explaining why he had finally decided to make the run. Here is some of what he said:

> After working for years as a citizen advocate for consumers, workers, taxpayers, and the environment, I am seeking the Green Party's nomination for president. A crisis of democracy in our country convinces me to take this action. Over the past twenty years, big business has increasingly dominated our political economy. This control by the corporate government over our political government is creating a widening "democracy gap". . . . This state of affairs is a world away from the legislative milestones in civil rights, the environment, and worker and consumer health and safety of the sixties and seventies. At that time, informed and dedicated citizens powered their concerns through the channels of government to produce laws that saved and bettered the lives of millions of Americans. One clear sign of the current reign of corporations over our government is that today those laws would not even pass through congressional committees. . . .
>
> We face grave and growing societal problems in health care, education, labor, energy, and the environment . . . But our political

leadership has been hijacked by the corporations, and decisions are being made by the 22,000 corporate lobbyists and 9,000 political action committees pumping money into both Republican and Democratic coffers. Citizen advocates have no other choice but to close the democracy gap by direct political means. Only effective national political leadership will restore the responsiveness of government to its citizenry.

I have a personal distaste for the trappings of modern politics, in which incumbents and candidates daily extol their own inflated virtues, paint complex issues with trivial brushstrokes, and propose plans quickly generated by campaign consultants. But I can no longer stomach the systemic political decay that has weakened our democracy.

Consider the economy, which business commentators say could scarcely be better. If, instead of corporate yardsticks, we use human yardsticks to measure our performance as a nation . . . we find a stunning array of deplorable conditions that continue to prevail year after year. Among them:

- A majority of workers make less now, inflation adjusted, than in 1979.
- More than 20 percent of children grew up in poverty during the past decade, by far the highest percentage among comparable Western countries.
- The minimum wage is lower today, inflation adjusted, than in 1979.

- American workers are working longer and longer hours—on average an additional 163 hours per year compared to twenty years ago—with less time for family and community.

- Many full-time family farms cannot make a living in a market of giant buyer concentration and industrial agriculture [agribusiness].

- Our public works are crumbling, with decrepit schools and clinics, library closings, and antiquated mass transit.

- Corporate welfare programs, paid for largely by middle-class taxpayers and amounting to hundreds of billions of dollars per year, continue to rise along with government giveaways of taxpayer assets such as public forests, minerals, new medicines, and public airwaves.

- The number of Americans without health insurance grows every year—currently at 46 million, an increase of 30 percent since 1992.

- Millions of inner-city residents are living in inadequate housing or have been forced to live on the streets because of national policies that have created a shortage of more than 5.4 million badly needed, affordable housing units.

- Consumer debt is at an all-time high, totaling more than $6 trillion.

- Personal savings have dropped to record lows and personal assets are so low that Bill Gates's net worth is equal to that of the net assets of the poorest 120 million Americans combined.

- The tiny federal budgets for the public's health and safety continue to be grossly inadequate.
- Motor vehicle fuel efficiency averages are actually declining and, overall, energy conservation efforts have slowed, while renewable energy takes a back seat to fossil fuel and atomic power subsidies.
- Wealth inequality is greater than at any time since World War Two. The top one percent of the wealthiest people have more financial wealth than the bottom 90 percent of Americans combined, the worst inequality among all large Western nations.

It is permissible to ask, in the light of these astonishing shortcomings during a period of prosperity, what the state of our country would be should a recession or depression occur. . . .

The foundation of our campaign is to focus on active citizenship, to create fresh political movements that will displace the control of the Democratic and Republican parties, two apparently distinct political entities that feed at the same corporate trough. They are, in fact, simply the two heads of one political duopoly: the DemRep Party, which does everything it can to obstruct the beginnings of new parties, including raising ballot access barriers, entrenching winner-take-all voting systems, and thwarting participation in the debates at election times.

. . . As befits its name, the Green Party stands for the regeneration of American politics. The new populism that the party represents involves motivated, informed voters who comprehend that "freedom is participation in power," to quote the ancient Roman orator Cicero. When citizen participation flourishes, as this campaign will encourage it to do, human values can tame runaway commercial imperatives. . . .[7]

On June 25, Nader and his running mate, the Native American activist Winona LaDuke, won the Green Party nomination. Their campaign slogan: Government Of, By, and For the People—Not Monied Interests. In contrast to his 1996 efforts, Nader was totally committed to the 2000 campaign for the presidency. He told an interviewer:

This time I'm running a serious, deliberate campaign. . . . We're going to put 30 full-time organizers in the field, we're going to raise $5 million, we're going for matching funds— which takes $5,000 minimum in each of 20 states. We're running with citizen groups that are already on the ground. I'm going into all 50 states—addressing real issues in those states.[8]

We will stand with the people in West Virginia who are fighting the coal companies on the issue of mountaintop removal. We'll be on the side of the homeless in the homeless shelter controversy in Atlanta, where the business people want to squeeze out the shelters because they don't want their homeless visible. We will be supporting those who are fighting against incinerators in Ohio."[9]

Nader knew he couldn't win the 2000 presidential election, but he could accomplish several things: He could inspire citizens to become activists and demand government response. He could focus a spotlight on his assertion that big corporations had become the "paymasters" of both the Democratic and Republican parties, and that there was very little substantive difference between the two. He had a practical goal as well. If he could get 5 percent of the vote, the Green Party would be eligible for federal election funds in 2004.

Nader had in-depth positions on all the issues, many of which differed dramatically from those of the presidential frontrunners, Vice President Al Gore, Democrat, and Governor George W. Bush, Republican, as well as from the Reform Party candidate, Patrick J. Buchanan.

> *On Welfare:* "While President Clinton and the Congress have gutted the welfare system for poor people, no such top-down agenda has emerged for corporate welfare recipients. The savage attacks on imaginary 'welfare queens' have never been matched with denunciations of gluttonous corporate welfare kings."[10]

> *On Gun Control:* "Look at a weapon the way you look at a car. You have to know how to handle it. You should be licensed."[11]

> *On Prescriptions:* "Under a system of universal health care [which Nader proposes], low-income Medicare recipients would receive

prescriptions at no cost. Price restraints should be placed on all drugs, especially those developed with taxpayer money. Also, multiple licenses should be issued for those drugs in order to stimulate competition and bring prices down. Medicare authorities should negotiate lower drug prices, just like the Pentagon and the Veterans Administration are already doing."[12]

On Tax Reform: "If anyone needs convincing about the need for campaign finance and political reform, they need look no further than the Internal Revenue Code, which is riddled with calculated loopholes, exemptions, credits, accelerated depreciation schedules, deductions, and targeted exceptions. Well-heeled Washington lobbyists representing high-donor corporate interests facilitate back-room deals that save their clients millions. The taxpayers, of course, lose commensurate amounts."[13]

On Drugs: "Our failed war on drugs is endangering our communities, imperiling police, wasting tens of billions of dollars, and criminalizing what is a health problem. Instead of rehabilitation for drug addicts, the system fills our prisons—at $40,000 per prisoner—making the corporate prison industry even richer. We should decriminalize marijuana and treat the drug problem as a rehabilitation/health problem."[14]

On Defense: [On the October 1, 2000, edition of *Meet The Press*, moderator Tim Russert asked Nader the following question: "The Green Party proposes cutting the defense budget in half. What programs would you cut to reduce spending by $150 billion?"]

"Bring back the troops from Western Europe and East Asia who, fifty-five years after World War II, are defending prosperous allies who can defend themselves against nonexistent enemies. That's $70 billion right there. Cancel those gold-plated weapons systems that ex-admirals, generals, and some Pentagon analysts say are not strategically needed: the F-22, the Joint Strike Fighter, another batch of Seawolf submarines, and the Osprey fighter, which has killed 34 Marines. . . . Streamline the procurement budget. Do what needs to be done to create a lean, effective military defense driven by defense considerations, not by the profit demands of Lockheed Martin, General Dynamics and others."[15]

On the Department of Defense: "No government agency is cozier with industry than the Department of Defense, and corporate welfare is pervasive at this agency, which is famous for cost overruns, waste, fraud, and abuse."[16]

On the Death Penalty: "In study after study, the death penalty has been shown not to deter homicides. It has also been shown to be discriminatorily applied to the poor and the defenseless, especially to defendants who don't have lawyers who can stay awake at trial."[17]

> ***On the Budget Surplus:*** "First of all, the sur-
> pluses are very hypothetical. The economy
> could turn down. [Nader said this on the
> October 1, 2000, *Meet The Press* telecast.]
> Second, the surpluses include a lot of Social
> Security funds, which must be secured. Our
> priorities are: First, abolishing child poverty.
> Second, rebuilding and repairing America, the
> public works, the drinking water system,
> public transit, schools, clinics—these are all
> crumbling. And third, we need to focus on
> universal health insurance that is accessible
> to all and puts its emphasis on prevention."[18]

Nader ran an articulate and well-informed campaign in
election year 2000. He had researched and mastered the
facts; he knew the statistics and the history behind
every issue. In October alone, he issued forty-four different statements, position papers, or press releases on
substantive issues ranging from land mines to stadiums
to affordable housing. Many of them were provocative,
even combative. All were, at the very least, thought-pro-
voking, bringing a uniquely Nader approach to each
problem.

∾∾∾

Unlike other candidates, Nader did not strive to "stay
on message" on any given day. He was more than
capable of speaking on any subject at any time. But no
one was asking him anything—at least not the members of the national press corps. From his February
announcement through mid-October, Nader was prac-
tically invisible in the popular media. He called it a
"media blackout," observing that six large multina-
tional conglomerates controlled more than half of all

mass media in the United States in 2000. "Our democracy is being swamped by the confluence of money, politics, and concentrated media," he said.[19] Nader didn't believe it was mere coincidence that the media outlets owned by those large corporations chose not to cover his campaign.

Ben Bagdikian, author of *The Media Monopoly* and former head of the Journalism School of the University of California at Berkeley, agreed that there might have been a media bias against Nader because of his anti-corporate stance. "I think there is a natural hostility among corporate organizations toward Nader," he says, "because he has embarrassed them endlessly and sees them as a part of the national political problem."[20]

Most journalists bristle at the idea that corporate owners dictate campaign coverage. "I guess if we sensed that the public was really clamoring for more about Nader we would have given it to them," says *Los Angeles Times* political researcher Maffie Ritsch. "But this entire campaign has been a two-person race and a very close one at that . . . and most people seem to be content with the two choices they have."[21]

Los Angeles Times Washington Bureau Chief Doyle McManus, a member of the Committee of Concerned Journalists, spoke on CNN's *Reliable Sources* on October 29. "Are you going to go out and spend a lot of time covering someone whose own supporters will admit he really doesn't have a chance of winning this thing. . . ?[22]

Jeff Cohen, a founder of the media watchdog group Fairness and Accuracy in Reporting (FAIR), analyzed media coverage in the presidential race and was surprised to learn that Gore had at least thirty major stories for every one on Nader. "Gore certainly doesn't have thirty times the support that Nader has," says

Cohen. "I'm not naïve, but this has shocked me—that a person this famous and respected should get this little coverage." At the time, Nader's support in the polls was at 5 percent, Gore's was between 40 and 45 percent, a ratio of eight or nine to one.[23]

According to Tom Squitieri, a national political correspondent for *USA Today*: "Reporters did not recognize . . . that Nader is unlike any other candidate in the sense that he has national renown and a track record as a reformer. He is talking about issues that the other candidates don't bring up, and those issues really resonate with a lot of voters. Nader has a consumer record unmatched by any member of Congress . . . if he had that record and had been a member of Congress, he would have gotten covered."[24] Nader was also the only candidate named by *Life* magazine as one of the 100 most influential people of the twentieth century.[25]

According to the Center for Media and Public Affairs, ABC, CBS, and NBC combined gave Nader only one minute of speaking time on their network evening news from Labor Day to October 22. Gore received twenty-three minutes, and Bush twenty-two.[26] During that same period, Nader's own research showed that the networks had 211 stories featuring Gore, 214 featuring Bush, and only four stories on his candidacy. That was less than 1 percent of the coverage despite the fact that his national poll numbers were running between 4 percent and 8 percent and reached 10 percent in some West Coast pockets and 17 percent in Alaska.[27] A Pew Research Center poll on October 20 showed him with 12 percent of undecided or "swing" voters who were classified as "attentive," meaning they heard and/or read a good deal about campaign issues.

The lack of media coverage is even harder to understand in light of the huge crowds that Nader's youth-driven campaign attracted as he barnstormed across the country. On August 26, he kicked off the first in a series of eight "Super Rallies" in Portland, Oregon. It was the largest political rally of the election year, with 10,500 people making $7 contributions to hear him speak. "Imagine that," said Nader's campaign manager Theresa Amato. "What other candidate would attempt to fill an arena while asking for donations in order to attend?"[28] Nader would break his own rally attendance record later in New York City.

The rallies regularly drew enthusiastic audiences of 10,000 or more, and Nader and his running mate were joined by celebrity supporters such as former talk-show host Phil Donahue, filmmaker Michael Moore, Eddie Vedder of Pearl Jam, author Studs Terkel, actor Danny Glover, and rock star Patti Smith. The local press covered the events, but the fact that a tall, slightly stooped sixty-six-year-old man in a dark suit could talk for forty minutes about serious issues and energize tens of thousands of mostly young people was a phenomenon that never caught the attention of the national media.

The largest rally took place in New York's Madison Square Garden on October 13 when more than 15,000 people heard Nader welcome them "to the politics of joy and justice." Phil Donahue hosted the evening and was joined by Eddie Vedder, Patti Smith, and actors Susan Sarandon, Tim Robbins, and Bill Murray. Reporting for NewsForChange.com, an online news service, Jennifer Bleyer wrote: "Madison Square Garden was packed with mostly young people—from teens through thirties. The only empty seats were the corporate skyboxes lining the third tier of the Garden." People had contributed $20 each to get in. But even with a boisterous, sellout crowd in its own backyard, *The New York Times* did not have even one of its own reporters cover the event. Instead,

At a Nader 2000 rally at Madison Square Garden, the Green Party presidential candidate gives a victory sign as the confetti flies.

the paper ran a 400-word story written by a reporter for the Associated Press (AP), a wire service.[29]

But a *New York Times* columnist, Gail Collins, did write about a Nader rally she attended in Madison, Wisconsin, where another sellout crowd of mostly young people paid $10 each to hear Nader—whom she calls the "nation's nag"—explain why he was running for president. She wrote: "The Republican and Democratic tickets probably could not get this kind of youthful turnout if they paid the audience."[30]

Nader's campaign contrasted sharply with those of the two leading candidates who traveled aboard their own jet planes surrounded by aides, handlers, pollsters, tutors, gofers, and scores of reporters. Nader ran a very lean campaign. His "entourage" consisted of his nephew Tarik. The two of them traveled on regularly scheduled flights—by coach. They rented a van, sometimes two, at each campaign stop. Nader preferred to stay at Hampton Inns. "A lot of reporters thought that was funny," says Jennifer Bleyer, the NewsForChange.com reporter who traveled with Nader for about six weeks. "I liked the fact that he stayed at the Hampton Inns—he was practicing what he was preaching. Besides, he didn't take very good care of himself. He would work an eighteen- or twenty-hour day, and if someone didn't put food in front of him, he would forget to eat. At the Hampton Inns there were free breakfast buffets set up so he would remember to eat."[31] For most of Bleyer's six weeks with Nader, she was the only reporter traveling with him.

The "Catch 22" analogy was often used to explain Nader's lack of media coverage. It went like this: If a candidate is low in the polls, he gets no media coverage. But he is low in the polls because he gets no media coverage. The same reasoning was used to keep him out of the three televised debates organized by the bipartisan (Democratic/Republican) Commission on Presidential Debates (CPD). Even though a majority of Americans told pollsters that they wanted Nader in the debates, the committee's self-imposed rules allowed only those candidates with national support of 15 percent to participate. Of course, the television networks could have hosted debates without the approval of the debate commission, but they chose not to do so.

At the first debate on October 3 in Boston, the commission even barred Nader from taking a seat in the viewing room, which was separate from the presidential debate auditorium at the University of Massachusetts. He had a legitimate ticket that had been given to him by a student earlier in the day, but he was turned away at the door by a security guard and three state troopers. Outside, five thousand Nader supporters rallied throughout the evening demanding that he be allowed to join the debate. His exclusion became a major part of his speeches, and future audiences took up the cry of "Let Ralph Debate" at almost every campaign event.

∾∾∾

Suddenly, in mid-October, Nader began to get media attention. But not to talk about the issues, only about the race itself.

It was a "horse race"—with Bush and Gore almost evenly divided in the polls just three weeks before the election. The Democrats and the media determined that the race was close because of Ralph Nader and called for him to withdraw and throw his support to Gore. Nader's 4 to 8 percent would give Gore a comfortable lead.

When Nader refused to step aside and throw his support to Gore, the press and the Democrats called him a "spoiler." "You can't spoil a system that's already spoiled to the core," Nader shot back.[32]

The New York Times ran a second editorial on October 26 (the first was on June 30) dismissing Nader's candidacy, echoing the "spoiler" theme, and calling his campaign "willful prankishness . . . a disservice to the electorate."

Nader wrote back: "You discredit our democracy by editorializing that the limited ground covered by the Gore and Bush candidacies should define political competition in this election. Millions of voters, when they contrast actual records to rhetoric, find the two major party candidates similar on excessive corporate power over our government. . . . You miss the point: we seek long-term political reform through a growing party that pushes the two parties toward the reforms that you have espoused over the years."[33]

Democratic Party leaders continued to call upon Nader to step down or, at least, encourage his supporters to vote for Gore in states where the race was very close. A dozen "Nader's Raiders for Gore" urged him to reassess his campaign. "It is now clear that you might well give the White House to Bush," the group wrote in an open letter to Nader.[34]

The press was now very interested in what Nader had to say, but only about the "horse race," his role as the spoiler, and his response to Democrats who were openly trying to dissuade liberals from supporting him. "Their [the Democrats'] policy for seven months has been to ignore me," replied Nader. "So obviously we welcome this enhanced attention."[35]

He tried, usually in vain, to turn the media's newfound interest in him into an opportunity to discuss the issues, and explain the differences between himself and the frontrunners. But the reporters were on just one track, and that involved the "horse race."

To those who said he was hurting Gore's chances, Nader responded: "He's taking votes away from me. Why should I entitle Gore to votes he doesn't deserve?" He admitted that he was disappointed that some progressive Democrats, including labor leaders and environmentalists, were Gore supporters. "They are defining their support of Gore by saying that Bush is so much worse," he says.[36]

Many Democrats took exception to Nader's contention that there was little difference between Gore and Bush. "What about appointments to the Supreme Court?" they asked. Conservative Bush appointees could reverse *Roe* v. *Wade* (the 1973 Supreme Court decision that declared unconstitutional state laws prohibiting all abortions except for those performed to save a woman's life). Nader replied that he didn't believe Republicans would ever overturn *Roe* v. *Wade*. "I think they would destroy their party if they pushed this to the limit. They are already very cautious about not taking a hard stand because they know they are going to lose a lot of votes if they do." He said he believed that the Republican Party's opposition to abortion was "just for show."[37]

Nader, of course, did not step down, nor did he encourage any of his supporters to vote for Gore. But the last-minute campaign to discredit him was effective. He estimates that it cost him millions of votes. Although he kept encouraging people not to vote out of fear for the "lesser of two evils," his support dropped to just under 3 percent by November 7, election day.

Chapter Eight "The birthpangs of a reform movement"

〜〜〜Nader fell short of his 5 percent goal, but for him and the Green Party, election day 2000 was a time for celebration. They had exceeded their $5 million fund-raising goal by nearly $3 million, they had been on the ballots in forty-four states, and had mobilized 150,000 volunteers—most of them young and enthusiastic. They had begun five hundred new local Green groups across the country and attracted a million new voters. Their Super Rallies had drawn the largest crowds of the political season. In addition, they had emerged as the third-largest political party in the United States, replacing Pat Buchanan and the Reform Party, which received less than 0.5 percent of the vote even though they outspent Nader and the Greens by close to $5 million.

The Green Party took no soft money (funds that are not subject to the rules of the Federal Election Campaign Act and that are given to the party rather than to specific candidates). Nor did it take money from corporations or Political Action Committees (PACs). "We rejected these funds because we wanted to set an example of what is necessary for real reform of our corrupt campaign system," Nader said.[1]

The Green Party's nearly $8 million in contributions came from individuals and averaged less than $100 each. "Nader's irreverent, youth-driven campaign spent less money [during the entire campaign] than the two major parties spent on television commercials during a typical week in October," wrote James Dao in *The New York Times* on November 11, 2000.

In contrast to Nader's $8 million, the Federal Election Commission reported that the Democrats raised $513 million ($243.1 of it in soft money) and the Republicans $691.8 million ($244.4 in soft money) during the 2000 election cycle.[2] The combined amounts represented a 37 percent increase over the 1996 presidential cycle; most of the increase was in soft money.

Theresa Amato, Nader's campaign manager, told columnist Micah L. Sifry that Nader had presented his agenda for a working democracy in all fifty states—as promised. "We were the only campaign talking about issues like the death penalty, fair trade, campaign finance reform, universal health care, and media concentration. And, we raised awareness of the corrupt Commission on Presidential Debates, filed two lawsuits against it, and brought nine lawsuits seeking to open up state ballot access."[3]

"It's an honorable list," Sifry agreed. "Nader ran a serious campaign that carried forward the torch of reform lit earlier in the year by Republican John McCain. He added his own distinct anticorporate critique and challenged many Americans to consider the stake in fostering a deep democracy."

Nader was clearly pleased with the campaign results, as was the enthusiastic crowd of campaign workers and supporters gathered at the National Press Club in Washington, D.C., on election night. "We've begun to build a long-term progressive reform movement," he told them, "and that takes commitment from people who are no longer willing to settle for the 'least of the worst' or the 'lesser of two evils,' because at the end of the day they know they are still stuck with worst and evil."[4]

He noted that David Broder, the political columnist for *The Washington Post*, had written that "hands down the Nader/LaDuke campaign was the best run in the 2000 election year."[5]

"We really practiced what we preached," Nader said. "Not just in the way we raised our funds, but in the way we comported ourselves, focusing on one important issue after another . . . which the Gore and Bush look-alike campaigns ignored, as did the media, which continued to pepper us with the horse race and spoiler questions."[6]

∾∾∾

The questions about Nader's role as the spoiler turned more openly hostile as election night wore on. The results nationwide were extremely close—the count in the state of Florida would decide the final outcome. But a series of ballot irregularities and confusion in the tabulation process necessitated a recount—first mechanically and, when that proved inconclusive, a recount by hand. One thing was certain, however. If all the Florida voters for Nader had voted for Gore, the vice president would have carried the state.

The Democrats, the leaders of progressive and liberal groups, and the media pundits went on the attack.

AFL–CIO president John Sweeney called Nader's campaign "reprehensible," and Democratic Party strategist James Carville said, "I'm going to shun him. And any good Democrat . . . ought to do the same thing." "He's totally toast," said a senior Democratic congressional aide.[7]

Meanwhile, the Florida vote recount continued in a series of starts and stops, lawsuits, court rulings, complaints, and cries of "foul play" from both Democrats and Republicans. Florida election officials struggled with a torturous examination of each ballot cast. The process lurched along for thirty-five days—which gave "blame Nader" forces a lot of time to seethe. Finally, on December 12, with George W. Bush leading by fewer than 600 votes, the United States Supreme Court called a halt to the vote counting.[8] Bush would be the forty-third president of the United States. The Gore backers were furious.

Nader, however, remained unfazed by the animosity directed toward him. He refused to accept the blame for Gore's loss, and maintained that any blame should be spread around.

"There are many so-called spoilers," he said. "There is the state of Tennessee (Gore's home state), the state of Arkansas (President Clinton's home state), and the traditionally Democratic state of West Virginia. Then there is the Democratically controlled county of Palm Beach, Florida, which didn't recount its votes in time for the Supreme Court cutoff. And how about George Bush? He took 10 times the number of Democratic votes in Florida than I did."[9]

Actually, according to journalist Tim Wise writing for *AlterNet* on the day after the election, Bush received twelve times more Democratic votes than Nader did in Florida, as well as 5.25 times more self-identified liberals than Nader.[10]

In an article entitled "Why Nader Is Not to Blame," Wise argues that the notion that Nader voters would have all voted for the vice president if Nader had not been on the ballot is "nonsense." "CNN exit polls showed that only about 47 percent of the Nader voters would have voted for Gore in a two-way race, while 21 percent would have voted for Bush and 30 percent would have abstained from voting in the presidential contest altogether. This is significant," Wise writes, "especially in New Hampshire and Oregon, where some are saying the Nader vote was the difference." [11]

Nader doesn't appear too concerned about the possibility of being frozen out by the Democratic Party. "Ties with most Democratic legislators haven't been there for a long time, " he says. "They said no to us on NAFTA (North American Free Trade Agreement), on the WTO (World Trade Organization)—(two international trade issues that Nader believes to be unfair to American workers)—the deregulation of the telecommunications industry, the merger craze, trade with China, automobile safety, stiffer food inspections, campaign finance reform, and universal health care. After a while, you get the idea." [12]

Perhaps the fractured Nader/Democratic Party relationship is not completely irreparable. In February 2001, House minority leader Richard Gephardt invited Nader in for what was described as a friendly visit. Nader says that Gephardt told him he disapproved of the harsh comments being made by many Democrats, and complimented him on his campaign, especially the impressive rallies that people paid to attend.

Columnist William Greider, writing in *The Nation*, observed: "Under the circumstances, it seems wiser for the Democrats to talk than to shun . . . Nader and the Greens . . . might be a useful asset, a force for stoking popular resistance to the party's rightward drift, drawing new voters and energy into the electoral process, test-marketing advanced issues that Democrats are still afraid to touch, perhaps even encouraging party discipline."[13] And Robert Reich, a prominent Democrat and former labor secretary in the Clinton administration, said that with Nader and the Green Party "we are witnessing the birth pangs of a reform movement in America intent on ending the corruption of our democratic system by money."[14]

Which is exactly what Ralph Nader was all about in 2001, although it was sometimes difficult for him to get his messages out. In February, for example, more than three months after the election, a reporter asked Nader why he had been so quiet and what he had been doing since the election.[15] Before he launched into the substantial list of his current projects, he couldn't help chiding her, saying: "Most of the coverage we have received was about the horse race. Now that the horse race has gone away, our coverage has gone away, because the mainstream press isn't interested in talking about real issues. We have had nine press conferences since the election, but [the public] hasn't heard much about them." The reporter went on to ask him thirteen more questions; more than half of them were about the horse race and his role as the spoiler.

Nader resumed his busy schedule after the 2000 election. He still worked long days—"I never count the hours I work. . . . I get up and I work, with breaks for food, until midnight. I sleep six or so hours a day."[16] He continued to accept speaking engagements—about a hundred a year, to write a weekly newspaper column, and was writing a book about the campaign. His post-election focus concentrated in three broad areas: building the Green Party, corporate reform, and promoting a prodemocracy agenda.

On the Green Party front, Nader believes that the party can broaden its influence and attract support in nonelection years by joining with activist groups concerned with local or regional issues, such as the homeless shelters in Atlanta and the incinerators in Ohio that he highlighted in his presidential campaign. He planned to establish several Green organizations—an educational group, a lobbying arm, and a political-action committee, similar to the successful citizen activist groups he launched in the 1970s, many of which still exist. He was considering setting up Green Party storefront operations in poor neighborhoods that would serve as "advice centers" to help people get assistance through Medicaid and other existing government programs.[17]

Nader hoped to have nine hundred Campus Green groups in action before the 2004 presidential election. Although he was unsure whether he would run for president again, he said: *"If* we run, we will need many more young people involved, because they're the ones that have the energy to do door-to-door canvassing. We were very gratified by the large number of young people who supported us in 2000, but there just weren't enough of them."[18] The Green Party would look for candidates to run in upcoming local, state, and national elections. He planned to establish a People's Debate Commission to counter the corporate-funded Commission on Presidential Debates, which barred him and other candidates from participation in the 2000 television debates.

Nader continues to tackle the large and complex issues of corporate power and weakening government, a combination that he believes thwarts the public interest. Early in 2001, California experienced a severe energy crisis, with rolling blackouts or brownouts imposed on the public to conserve power; the state's two largest utility companies said they faced bank-ruptcy. Nader publicly urged President George W. Bush to intervene in the crisis, saying that the administration should regulate the wholesale price of electricity in the western United States in order to control the rates of electricity for consumers. He also accused the president of using the California power crisis to drum up support for oil drilling in the Arctic National Wildlife Refuge, which Bush endorses and most environmentalists oppose.

Nader also weighed in on the issue of e-commerce. Rather than singling out any one corporation, he targeted the entire e-commerce industry. He said the Internet is the ideal vehicle for massive consumer fraud and likens it to "a runaway train with no conductor."[19]

He called for the formation of a World Consumer Protection Organization (WCPO), which would oversee Internet governance, e-commerce, intellectual property, and online privacy. The goal of the new organization would be to counter threats posed by increased global trade and Internet-based fraud. In making his proposal public, Nader cited a recent Harris Poll showing that six million Americans felt they had been defrauded online in the past year.

"The technology of the Internet is way ahead of any legal framework, or any ethical framework, or any public awareness," Nader said. "It enables con artists to defraud consumers on a greater scale across international borders, so nations need to forge treaties that would regulate electronic commerce, protect privacy and encourage competitive markets."[20]

Nader also continues to battle what he considers to be an unholy alliance between two Goliaths—one corporate, the other governmental. Early in 2001 he pointed to what he considers a textbook example of corporate welfare: New York City and New York State granted a host of subsidies totaling more than $1 billion to the New York Stock Exchange (NYSE) in an effort to keep it from moving out of the state.

In February, Nader summed up the situation in an open letter to Mayor Rudolph Giuliani and Governor George Pataki:

> The NYSE has agreed to accept a gift of a new building and other benefits from the City and State. The arrangement commits the City to acquire a plot of land for the new exchange, and for the City and State to construct a new luxurious trading floor for the NYSE, grant substantial tax benefits to the NYSE, and make discount energy available to the NYSE. This boondoggle is likely to cost taxpayers nearly $1.1 billion ($450 million for land acquisition, $480 million for construction, and $160 million in tax and utility cost breaks).
>
> You are conferring staggering taxpayer benefits on a private entity without any conceivable public benefit. No one can possibly believe that the NYSE, if in fact it needs a new trading floor, could not raise sufficient funds from its member firms. . . .
>
> The sole purported rationale for this corporate welfare bonanza is to retain the New York Stock Exchange in New York City. This gift of more than $1 billion to retain fewer than 5,000 jobs would, even by the corrupt standards of job-retention blackmail deals, set a high-water mark for ransom payments among arrangements of this scale. The City and State

are receiving nothing in return for the windfall they are bestowing on the NYSE. Although it is true that the NYSE chairman has blustered a threat to move to New Jersey, there is no chance—none, zero—that the stock exchange would leave New York City. The Jersey City Stock Exchange? Be serious. . . .

Surely some residual sense of shame must persist in New York politics. In a state with one of the nation's worst child poverty rates, and one of the largest gaps between rich and poor, is a billion-dollar subsidy for the bastion of global capitalism not beyond the pale?[21]

Vintage Nader.

∽∾∽

Nader enjoys his work. He says he learned long ago that if something is important, you enjoy doing it. "That way," he says, "you don't have to fight with yourself every day."[22]

He has been called a recluse, an aesthete, a grind, and a workaholic. He is frequently scorned for his austere, disciplined lifestyle. "I don't have a lifestyle," he says, "I have a *work*style." He seems genuinely surprised that some people find his dedication and commitment puzzling. "Is it so implausible, so distasteful, that a man would believe deeply enough in his work to dedicate his life to it?" he asks.[23]

But he doesn't always work. Long-time acquaintances in Connecticut say that when he visits family in Winsted, he attends social functions and is a charming and entertaining guest as well as a gracious and witty host. But they know that before and after the party, Nader is hard at work. "It runs in the family," says Sally Hannafin, a public relations consultant who has known

From left to right, the Naders—Claire, Ralph, Laura, and Rose—enjoy a festive evening with old friends Larry and Sally Hannafin in the Hannafin's home in Norfolk, Connecticut.

the Naders for many years and was a patron of the Naders' Highland Arms Restaurant. "They are all thinkers, always dedicated to an issue. You're not a member of that family unless you're marching to some mission. Their lives are living civics lessons. And it's contagious when you are around them."[24]

"He's America's cheerleader," adds her husband, Larry Hannafin, formerly Director of the Real Estate Division of Connecticut's Department of Consumer Protection. "He is always trying to get the rest of America to do something to make the country better."[25]

And he is never more effective at that than when he is addressing groups of young people.

Chapter Nine "A better place than when he entered"

ᴥᴥᴥIt is a clear, cold afternoon several months after election 2000. In Washington, D.C., George W. Bush is in the White House. Just across the Potomac River in northern Virginia, some six hundred young men and women are gathered in a hotel ballroom. They are members of the Junior State of America, a nationwide organization of high-school students with a special interest in current events, politics, and government. The organization's stated purpose is to improve education, promote democracy, and learn about government through participation. This is an audience made for Ralph Nader.

Unlike the 2000 campaign rallies, there are no rockers, no celebrities, no music. No glitz, no glamour, no chants of "Let Ralph Debate." Nader is about ten minutes late, and while they wait, these high schoolers chat with one another about the morning's program and events scheduled for later in the day. It is a no-nonsense kind of crowd.

When Nader arrives and a Junior Statesman wearing a dark suit and tie introduces him as "one of the great American heroes of the twentieth century," the young crowd comes alive. They give him a standing ovation as he takes the podium. He acknowledges the welcome with a shy smile. He is also wearing a dark suit and tie, as usual. "Ralph's cool," says one Junior State member to his neighbor.

Nader opens with a question: "Did you speak with members of Congress yet?" When they answer in the affirmative, he says, "Well, now we'll have to unspeak you."

He talks about his issues—abuse of corporate power, citizen empowerment, civic responsibility. He makes no attempt to "talk down" to the students. He says he never does, because young people can and have made significant contributions to democracy, citing their role in ending the Vietnam War, gaining environmental protections, and enacting civil-rights legislation.

He tells his audience that American students are in the top 2 percent of their age group worldwide in terms of health, education, and the ability to make a difference, noting that the primary concern of millions of teenagers is finding their next meal.

He believes that this generation of young people can change the world, if they so choose. He asks who among them will save the forests, who will make the government work better, who will solve the problems of the health-care delivery system. To impress them with the need to become active sooner rather than later, he tells them, "You only have about 17,000 days until you reach age 65, only 2,400 weeks to retirement. And didn't last week go by fast?"

He tells the students to be wary of the corporate culture in which they have grown up. "Corporations know

Nader speaks to students at a Junior State of America conference in 2001.

how to tap into your minds, your bodies, and your sense of loneliness. You grew up looking at things the corporations wanted you to look at. They even define beauty for you, and that often causes you to be cruel to each other. Too many young people lose 30 to 40 hours out of their lives each week to the market system by watching television."

He tells them that the major corporations could solve the problems of starvation in the world and cure recurring diseases like TB and malaria. "Ask yourself this about corporations," he says. "To what degree are they solving the world's problems, or worsening the world's problems, or being indifferent to the world's problems?"

He speaks the words: crime . . . violence . . . welfare. "Most people associate these words with poor inner cities," he says. "Not so. There is far more crime, violence, and welfare in the corporate world than there is in the impoverished street arena. Air pollution takes 50,000 lives a year, 100,000 lives are lost due to toxins and accidents in the workplace, 65,000 people die of malpractice by doctors and hospitals, and 420,000 are lost due to smoking tobacco. In the case of smoking, the corporation is the addictor since tobacco companies try to hook youngsters into a lifetime of smoking between the ages of ten and fifteen. Those same companies are now busy luring millions of Asians and Africans into a lifetime of smoking."

Nader talks about the corporate-welfare programs provided by the federal government. He tells them about New York's "boondoggle" of subsidies to the New York Stock Exchange, and draws laughter when he asks: "Can you believe a Jersey City Stock Exchange?" (This particular group of Young States members are from the Northeast region.)

Nader explains how taxpayers are being abused by the big pharmaceutical companies. "There's a drug called Taxol that fights ovarian cancer," he says. "That drug was produced by a grant of $31 million of taxpayer money through the National Institutes of Health, right through the clinical testing process. The formula was then given away to a major pharmaceutical company. No royalties were paid to the taxpayer. There was no restraint on the price, so patients pay between $10,000 and $15,000 each for the required series of treatments. If the patients can't pay, they go on Medicaid, which is paid for by the taxpayers. So the taxpayers pay at both ends, and the corporation reaps the benefits. This is not an isolated incident."

The fact that most people do not know about corporate welfare or recognize corporate abuses that affect the health or safety of the public means, to Nader, that they "grew up corporate."

"When you grow up corporate," he explains, "you are not alerted to civic alternatives. Civic responsibility is more than charitable activities. Working at a soup kitchen is a worthwhile act, but you should be asking: '*Why* are there so many hungry people?' More justice means less charity."

Nader asks the students if they could make a list of their civic skills. They give him a blank stare, and that makes his point. "You have academic skills, athletic skills, people skills, but you have no array of civic skills because we don't teach civic skills in our schools." He challenges them to develop and exercise their civic skills, recommending a book, *More Action for Change*, a primer on organizing citizen activism that he wrote several years ago, and encourages them to go to his Web site, essential.org, to learn more about the dozens of grassroots organizations that harness citizen action on a wide variety of national and international issues— from the ozone to banking to advertising. He tells these young people to begin to think about their legacy— what they will leave for the generations that follow. He reminds them of a pledge taken by citizens of ancient Athens: "I will leave Athens a better place than when I entered it."

By the time he finishes his chock-full-of-facts-and-figures thirty-minute address, about fifty students are already lined up behind a floor microphone with questions. There are one or two "spoiler" questions, which he answers patiently—he has had a lot of practice with spoilers. But most of the questions are serious and well-thought-out.

He is running late—a chronic condition with Nader—but he continues to answer questions long past the allotted fifteen minutes. Then he makes his way through the crowd and takes his place behind a table piled with copies of *The Ralph Nader Reader,* a collection of his speeches and writings on dozens of issues spanning more than thirty years. About one hundred young people buy the book and wait in line to get his autograph. Nader is relaxed, obviously comfortable talking with them. He gets their names, writes personal inscriptions in their books, and answers questions— "It's too soon to say" (Will you run again?) and "It's only a single when what we need is a home run" (What do you think about the McCain/Feingold legislation for campaign-finance reform?) Smiling, he poses for pictures and banters with those who have brought cameras, and many have. He is now running more than an hour late, and George, his aide for the day, is busy on his cell phone trying to assure those waiting at his next stop that he is on the way.

It is nearly sunset by the time Nader heads back across the 14th Street Bridge to Washington. Intending to give a thirty-minute speech, he has now spent three hours with these young people. The following week, he will give a similar address to twice as many members of Junior State from the Southeast region. He has probably made more speeches to America's youth, on and off college campuses, over the previous thirty years than anyone else in history.

Nader believes that some members of this audience—or any audience of young people that he addresses—will go on to become citizen activists. It is events like these, or rallies or demonstrations, that light the fire, Nader says. "Of course, these young people will hear a thousand presentations from the other side, and most of them will be swallowed up by corporate society. But some, who may already have the inclination, can be moved forward by what we did here today."

Even more optimistically, he doesn't rule out another activist generation like that of the 1960s because "there will be more and more perceived calamities. AIDS is a calamity, the structure of the World Trade Organization will lead to calamities. When people start seeing the glaciers melting, and the tides running higher and higher, and more coastal land under water—that will wake them up. When they see that infectious diseases are once again on the rise and realize that more and more two-income families cannot make ends meet—then they will take action."

As he has been for nearly four decades, Ralph Nader is tireless in his efforts to help the citizenry take those actions. He believes there should be elementary and secondary school civics classes as well as adult education in civics at night in high schools and community colleges. "People have to learn that they can change things and stand up against the government and the corporations. They need to know that their forebears went up against great odds to change things—the abolitionists struggled against slavery; farmers fought large, oppressive railroads and banks; and trade unionists fought against brutal workplace conditions. And they did it without electricity, automobiles, telephones and Web sites."

Today's fight, as Nader sees it, is against corporate power and a collapsing democracy. "Everything," he says, "flows from that. All the issues we talk about—taxes, corporate welfare, bloated military budget, foreign policy, poverty, health—flow from the weakening of our civic institutions." Far from being intimidated by

a battle of this magnitude, Nader asks, "How can you not keep fighting?"

Has he made a difference? "I never look back," Nader says, "there's just too much to be done today and tomorrow."

☙ ☙ ☙

Listening to him speak, you can almost hear Rose and Nathra Nader at the family dinner table urging their children to ask questions, to get involved, to fix things that are wrong.

"We were all expected to accomplish things, to make a difference," says his sister Claire. "No one in our family thought there was anything unusual about what Ralph was doing. Still, when you stand back and look at his life, it is quite a road that he has traveled."

Nathra Nader, Ralph Nader's activist father, died in 1991. He was an inspiration to all of his children. Following are some of his more notable sayings, as reported by his children.

- Unless you have all the answers, why don't you have any questions?

- Don't separate your mind from your brain or let anyone else do that for you.

- In our society, people are grown old rather than grow old.

- Any country that rejects or abuses its truthsayers is sure to eventually turn them into prophets.

- Your best teacher is your last mistake, no tuition required.

- If you don't use your rights, you'll lose your rights.

- Watch out that your way of opposing your worst adversaries does not make you more like them. For if that happens, they have won.

- Colleges now teach students how to make a living instead of how to make a life.

- Don't look down on anyone and don't be in awe of anyone.

- Almost everyone will claim they love their country. If that is true, why don't they spend more time improving it?

- The mindless "we're first" mentality in America can be taken too far. It has gotten in the way of learning from other nations and cultures and makes us less likely to be sensitive to areas of life where we are neither first, nor second, nor third.

- Every time I hear the term "dumb animal," I have to laugh. "Dumb animals" do not smoke or drink, they don't kill their own, they don't wage organized war, they don't soil their own nest, and they don't watch television while they eat.

- When the rich get our tax money it's called a subsidy; when the poor get it, it's called welfare. Actually the rich are our biggest welfare cases.

- Elections are like auctions. Politicians trot themselves out daily to give a piece of themselves in return for campaign money.

- When politicians are engaged in bad deeds, they most often raise the flag and invoke God.

- People throughout history have responded more to leaders who have asked them to believe than to leaders who have asked them to think. . . .

- A necessary condition for the decline of any society is the widespread feeling among the people that "it can't happen here."

- Separate a politician from his smile and you're halfway home to knowing what he is really up to.

- There is an Arabic proverb that says: "If you're going to lie, be sure you have a good memory."

- Most politicians would rather be flattered than remembered. . . . Unfortunately, this is true for a sizable number of voters.

- Whenever we judge business, we should ask: Do these companies just seek temporary wealth for themselves or genuine wealth for society?

- Genuine patriotism is being pleased with how far our country has come and displeased with how far we have yet to go.

- Foresight is often a decision that pinches now but pleases later.

- You can be a slave if you do not have a dollar and another kind of slave if you have too many dollars.

From "It Happened in the Kitchen" by Rose B. Nader and Nathra Nader—copyright 1991 by Center for Study of Responsive Law (a Nader organization)

Chronology

1934	Born February 27 in Winsted, Connecticut
1955	Graduates from Princeton University
1958	Graduates from Harvard Law School; serves in the U.S. Army Reserves
1964	Accepts a job at the U.S. Department of Labor; moves to Washington, D.C.
1965	*Unsafe at Any Speed* is published
1966	General Motors chairman James Roche apologizes for investigating Nader
	National Traffic and Motor Vehicle Safety Act is passed
1968	First team of Nader's Raiders investigates the Federal Trade Commission
1969	Forms first of many public interest organizations, the Center for Study of Responsive Law (CSRL)
1970	Settles lawsuit with General Motors; uses money to found first Public Interest Research Group (PIRG)
1971	Founds Public Citizen, an umbrella organization that supports a variety of public interest activites
1974	Creates the Critical Mass Energy Project to oppose the growth of nuclear power
1978	Loses the battle to create a federal Consumer Protection Agency

1986   Contracts Bell's Palsy disease; brother Shafeek dies of cancer

1988   Successfully leads fight to roll back insurance rates in California

1991   Father Nathra dies

1992   Runs as independent candidate for president in the New Hampshire primary

1996   Accepts invitation of the Green Party to be its candidate for President; receives 700,000 votes

2000   Runs for President on the Green Party ticket; receives just under three million votes; Democrats blame him for Gore loss to Bush

Source Notes

INTRODUCTION

1. Robert F. Buckhorn, *Nader, The People's Lawyer* (Englewood Cliffs, NJ: Prentice-Hall, 1972), p. 19.
2. Buckhorn, p. 29

CHAPTER ONE

1. Author interview with Claire Nader, January 9, 2001.
2. Author interview with Claire Nader, January 9, 2001.
3. Author interview with Claire Nader, January 9, 2001.
4. Author interview with Claire Nader, January 9, 2001.
5. Robert F. Buckhorn, *Nader, The People's Lawyer* (Englewood Cliffs, NJ: Prentice-Hall, 1972), p. 19
6. Author interview with Claire Nader, January 9, 2001.
7. Author interview with Claire Nader, January 9, 2001.
8. Author interview with Claire Nader, January 9, 2001.
9. Author interview with Claire Nader, January 9, 2001.
10. Interview on *Alternative Radio* with David Barsamian, February 23, 2000.

CHAPTER TWO

1. Teresa Celsi, *Ralph Nader, The Consumer Revolution* (Brookfield, CT: The Millbrook Press, 1991).
2. Robert F. Buckhorn, *Nader, The People's Lawyer* (Englewood Cliffs, NJ: Prentice-Hall ,1972), p. 44.

3. Kevin Graham, *Ralph Nader, Battling for Democracy* (Denver, CO: Windom Publishing, 2000), p. 39.
4. Graham, p. 39.
5. Author interview with Claire Nader, January 9, 2001.
6. Buckhorn, *Nader*, p. 45.

CHAPTER THREE

1. Kevin Graham, *Ralph Nader, Battling for Democracy* (Denver, CO: Windom Publishing, 2000), p. 50.
2. Graham, p. 56.
3. Ralph Nader, *Unsafe at Any Speed* (New York, NY: Grossman Publishers, Inc., 1965), p. vi.
4. Nader, *Unsafe*.
5. Teresa Celsi, *Ralph Nader, The Consumer Revolution* (Brookfield, CT: The Millbrook Press, 1991), p. 12.
6. Celsi, p. 13.
7. Robert F. Buckhorn, *Nader, The People's Lawyer* (Englewood Cliffs, NJ: Prentice-Hall, 1972), p. 6.
8. Buckhorn, p. 5.
9. Buckhorn, p. 7.
10. Buckhorn, p. 9.
11. Buckhorn, p. 8.
12. Buckhorn, p. 16.
13. Buckhorn, p. 17.
14. Walter Rugaber, *The New York Times,* March 23, 1966, p. 1.
15. Buckhorn, p. 18.
16. Celsi, p. 38.
17. David Bollier, *Citizen Action and Other Big Ideas* (Washington, DC: Center for the Study of Responsive Law, 1991), p. 4.

CHAPTER FOUR

1. David Bollier, *Citizen Action an Other Big Ideas* (Washington, DC: Center for the Study of Responsive Law, 1991), p. 4.
2. Robert F. Buckhorn, *Nader, The People's Lawyer* (Englewood Cliffs, NJ: Prentice-Hall, 1972), p. 54.
3. Buckhorn, p. 37.
4. Buckhorn, p. 91.
5. Buckhorn, p. 87.
6. Buckhorn, p. 84.
7. Buckhorn, p. 87

8. *Contemporary Heroes and Heroines*, Book I (Detroit, MI: Gale Research, 1990).
9. Buckhorn, p. 110.
10. William Manchester, *Portrait of an American: Ralph Nader* © 1973,1974 by Wm. Manchester, p. 1257. www.nader96.org/rn1975.htm

CHAPTER FIVE

1. Robert F. Buckhorn, *Nader, The People's Lawyer* (Englewood Cliffs, NJ: Prentice-Hall, 1972), p. 54.
2. Buckhorn, p. 104.
3. Kevin Graham, *Ralph Nader, Battling for Democracy* (Denver, CO: Windom Publishing, 2000), p. 73.
4. Buckhorn, p. 126.
5. Buckhorn, p. 122.
6. David Bollier, *Citizen Action and Other Big Ideas* (Washington, DC: Center for the Study of Responsive Law, 1991), 6:1.
7. *The Ralph Nader Reader* (New York, NY: Seven Stories Press, 2000), p. 147
8. Graham, p. 79.
9. Graham, p. 79.
10. Bollier, 5:2.
11. Graham, p. 83.
12. Bollier, 5:2.
13. Bollier, 5:4

CHAPTER SIX

1. Kevin Graham, *Ralph Nader: Battling for Democracy* (Denver, CO: Windom Publishing, 2000), p. 95.
2. Author interview with Ralph Nader, February 17, 2001.
3. Author interview with Ralph Nader, February 17, 2001.
4. Graham, p. 95.
5. Author interview with Ralph Nader, February 17, 2001.
6. Author interview with Ralph Nader, February 17, 2001.
7. Author interview with Ralph Nader, February 17, 2001.
8. Author interview with Ralph Nader, February 17, 2001.
9. Author interview with Claire Nader, January 9, 2001.
10. Author interview with Ralph Nader, February 24, 2001.
11. Teresa Celsi, *Ralph Nader, The Consumer Revolution* (Brookfield, CT: The Millbrook Press, 1991), p. 92.

CHAPTER SEVEN

1. Author interview with Ralph Nader, February 24, 2001.
2. Kevin Graham, *Ralph Nader, Battling for Democracy* (Denver, CO: Windom Publishing, 2000), p. 106.
3. Graham, p. 107.
4. Author interview with Ralph Nader, February 24, 2001.
5. Author interview with Ralph Nader, February 24, 2001.
6. Author interview with Ralph Nader, February 24, 2001.
7. *The Ralph Nader Reader* (New York, NY: Seven Stories Press, 2000), p. 3.
8. Robert Kuttner, *The American Prospect*, June 19, 2000, p. 15.
9. Kuttner.
10. www.issues2000.com
11. www.issues2000.com
12. www.issues2000.com
13. www.issues2000.com
14. www.issues2000.com
15. www.issues2000.com
16. www.issues2000.com
17. www.issues2000.com
18. www.issues2000.com
19. Author interview with Ralph Nader, February 24, 2001.
20. Jennifer Bleyer, NewsForChange.com. November 1, 2000, p. 3.
21. Matt Welch, *Online Journalism Review*, November 3, 2000, p. 2.
22. Welch, p. 3.
23. Bleyer, p. 2.
24. Bleyer, p. 2.
25. 1990 *LIFE Magazine* special issue: "The 100 Most Important Americans of the Century."
26. Bleyer, p. 1.
27. Nader2000 Web site, October 30, 2000.
28. Nader2000 Web site, October 30, 2000.
29. Welch, p. 3.
30. Gail Collins, "The Last Angry Man," *The New York Times*, September 22, 2000, p. A27.
31. Author interview with Jennifer Bleyer, NewsForChange, February 28, 2001.
32. Quotation of the Day, *The New York Times*, July 1, 2000.
33. Letters to the Editor, *The New York Times*, October 29, 2000.

34. Associated Press, October 14, 2000.
35. Quotation of the Day, *The New York Times*, October 30, 2000.
36. *Business Week*, Issue 3700, September 25, 2000, p. 82.
37. www.issues2000.com

CHAPTER EIGHT

1. Ralph Nader, NewsForChange, November 8, 2000.
2. Federal Election Commission News Release, January 12, 2001.
3. Micah L. Sifry, NewsForChange.com, November 28, 2000.
4. Ralph Nader, NewsForChange, November 8, 2000.
5. Ralph Nader, NewsForChange, November 8, 2000.
6. Ralph Nader, NewsForChange, November 8, 2000.
7. David Corn, *The Nation*, December 4, 2000, p. 17.
8. Federal Election Commission, 2000 Official Presidential General Election Results, February, 8, 2001.
9. Evelyn Nieves, *The New York Times*, February 18, 2001, p. 7.
10. Tim Wise, "Why Nader Is Not To Blame," AlterNet, November 8, 2000.
11. Author interview with Ralph Nader, February 24, 2001.
12. William Greider, *The Nation*, March 12, 2001.
13. Sifry, p. 1.
14. Nieves, p. 7.
15. Author interview with Ralph Nader, February 24, 2001.
16. Corn, p. 17.
17. Author interview with Ralph Nader, February 24, 2001.
18. Paul A. Greenberg, EcommerceTimes.com, February 7, 2000.
19. Greenberg.
20. Author interview with Ralph Nader, February 17, 2001.
21. Open letter from Ralph Nader to Governor George Pataki, February 12, 2001, available at www.essential.org
22. Author interview with Ralph Nader, February 17, 2001.
23. Author interview with Ralph Nader, February 17, 2001.
24. Author interview with Sally Hannafin, February 2, 2001.
25. Author interview with Larry Hannafin, February 2, 2001.

For Further Information

BOOKS

Bollier, David. *Citizen Action and Other Big Ideas: A History of Ralph Nader and the Modern Consumer Movement.* Washington, D.C.: Center for the Study of Responsive Law, 1991.

Graham, Kevin. *Ralph Nader, Battling for Democracy.* Denver: Windom Publishing Company, 2000.

Nader, Ralph. *The Ralph Nader Reader.* New York: Seven Stories Press, 2000.

Nader, Ralph. *Unsafe at Any Speed: The Designed-In Dangers of the American Automobile.* New York: Grossman Publishing, 1965.

RELATED WEB SITES

www.essential.org
Contains links to a wide variety of citizen-action groups and projects, including Public Citizen, the Center for Auto Safety, the Death Penalty Information Center, the Congressional Accountability Project, Corporate Abuse, and The Nader Page.

www.nader.org
This Web site has current and past editions of "In the Public Interest," a weekly newspaper column written by Nader; *The Nader Letter*, his 8-page monthly newsletter; and news releases

and transcripts of Nader's testimony before various government bodies. It also contains the book, *Citizen Action and Other Big Ideas: A History of Ralph Nader and the Modern Consumer Movement*, written by David Bollier.

www.pirg.org
Provides information on the activities of state Public Interest Research Groups (PIRGs) as well as the national PIRG in Washington, D.C.

www.governmentguide.com
America On Line's list of all government agencies and services.

www.greenparty.org
Information about the Green Party and its activities.

www.publiccitizen.org
Contains Public Citizen reports on a variety of consumer issues and links to many issue-related data bases. Provides opportunities to register support or opposition to timely political and government matters.

Index